MYSTERIES

OF THE

TOWER OF LONDON

G. ABBOTT

Yeoman Warder (retd)
HM Tower of London
Member of Her Majesty's Bodyguard
of the
Yeomen of the Guard Extraordinary

D1316194

HENDON PUBLISHING : NELSON

Geoffrey Abbott joined the Royal Air Force in August 1939 as an aero-engine fitter. He saw active service in North and East Africa, Somalia and India; in the Suez Canal Zone, the Hashemite Kingdom of Jordan, Iraq, Cyprus, Malta and the Gulf States after World War II, and later served with Nato in France, Germany, and Holland. On leaving the RAF as a Warrant Officer in 1974 he joined the Body of Yeoman Warders, thereby being sworn in at St. James' Palace as a member of the Queen's Bodyguard of the Yeomen of the Guard Extraordinary, and lived with his wife Shelagh in Her Majesty's Tower of London. He now lives in the Lake District where he acts as consultant to TV and film companies and enjoys writing, visiting castles and being Sword Bearer to the Mayor of Kendal, Cumbria.

ISBN 0-86067-151-8

£5.80

9 780860 671510 >

Dedicated to
Yeoman Warder Brian Harrison and his wife Mary
my close friends for many years
and it is a Tower Mystery to me
how this book could ever have been written
without his valuable contributions!

ACKNOWLEDGEMENTS

Tributes are due to all those who assisted me in the compilation of this book, in particular Yeoman Warder Brian Harrison, Honorary Archivist of the Tower of London, for providing me with vital information from his extensive and unique records of those imprisoned in the Tower over the last nine hundred years, and to Dr. Geoff Parnell, Tower Archaeologist who, while I lived in the Tower, never failed to inform me of his many finds and then explained them. Thanks are also due to Mr Arthur D John of Redlands, California, for his permission to use the negative of the ghostly hand photographed at Traitors' Gate and especially to his daughter Shannon for pressing the camera release! I also thank my fellow residents, colleagues and members of the staff who reported their supernatural experiences to me and endured my subsequent cross-questioning to check authenticity! Nor should my close friends David and Jil Atkinson be forgotten; were it not for their encouragement when my word processor screen was as blank as my mind, these pages would be in a similar state!

CONTENTS

ILLUSTRATIONS

17th CENTURY PLAN OF THE TOWER OF LONDON

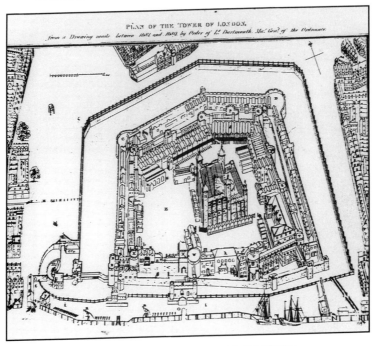

PLAN OF THE TOWER OF LONDON.
from a Drawing made between 1682 and 1688, by Order of L.ᵗ Dartmouth, Ma.ᵗ Gen.ˡ of the Ordnance.

LOCATIONS REFERRED TO IN TEXT

A   Martin Tower
B   Byward Tower
C   Legge's Mount
D   Brass Mount
F   Well Tower
G   Cradle Tower
H   Traitors' Gate
I   Drawbridge
K   Bell Tower
L   Beauchamp Tower
M   Devereux Tower
N   Flint Tower

O   Bowyer Tower
R   Constable Tower
T   Salt Tower
V   Lanthorn Tower
W   Wakefield Tower
X   Bloody Tower
Y   Chapel Royal of St Peter
Z   Tower Green
a   White Tower
b   Lieutenant's Lodgings
o   Tower Wharf

~ INTRODUCTION ~

One would have thought that after nine centuries or more, a place as important as Her Majesty's Royal Palace and Fortress the Tower of London, to give it its full title, could have no mysteries; so official were its many activities, so documented its many functions, that surely everything must have been reported or recorded, explained or accounted for. This was no little used government office block, no minor departmental headquarters; for centuries it was the most important collection of buildings in the country. All English history as we know it started at the Tower, an edifice older than the Kremlin and the Vatican, more ancient than Vienna's Burg or Paris's Palace of the Louvre. Not only did kings and queens preside over their royal courts here for hundreds of years, but the State Regalia and the Crown Jewels, the Royal Armouries, the Mint, the nation's treaty records and official papers were housed behind its battlemented walls. Arms for 100,000 men were stored in its arsenal and of course it was a State prison for those who plotted against the throne, a much-feared gaol equipped with ample means of persuading the most obstinate conspirator to divulge all he, or she, knew.

Yet despite its vital importance in the life of the nation and all the meticulous records maintained, the Tower's past is punctuated by question marks, its history inextricably and in many cases, inexplicably, intertwined with mystery. Not only does buried treasure await discovery and skeletons plead for identification, but the spirits of the hapless prisoners who died by bullet or blade, suffocation or poison, all cry out for the truth to be revealed, their killers named, the reasons for their cruel deaths exposed.

But as the following pages will show, dark are the shadows where the Tower's secrets lurk, and brave the person who seeks to unravel the threads of the past.

1. The Buried Treasure of Sir John Barkstead

Each day thousands of tourists visit the Tower with the intention of seeing the fabulous treasures displayed in the Jewel House, yet few if any are aware that within yards of where they pass, another treasure is believed to lie beneath the soil, buried there more than three hundred years ago by the then Lieutenant of the Tower, Sir John Barkstead.

At the outbreak of the Civil War in 1642 he was a goldsmith in the Strand and, seeing where his duty and no doubt his future pecuniary prospects lay, he joined those opposed to King Charles I, attaining the rank of captain of parliamentary infantry and later, as colonel, commanded a regiment at the siege of Colchester. In 1645 he became governor of Reading and after the cessation of hostilities the leaders of the newly established Commonwealth recognised his particular talents and selected him as one of the judges at the King's trial, thereby making him one of those directly responsible for the passing of the death sentence and subsequent execution of the monarch.

More honours followed. In 1649 he was given the post of Governor of Yarmouth and on 12 August 1652 he was appointed Lieutenant of the Tower of London, his income, together with his military pay as Major-General of London, then amounting to about £2000 a year, hardly an inconsiderable sum in those days. Coincidental with his duties in the City he became Member of Parliament for Colchester, and later for Middlesex, but probably the high point of his already glittering career occurred in 1656 when he was 'knighted' by Cromwell on being appointed Steward of the Protector's Household, a post which offered many lucrative opportunities to augment his bank balance even further by careful manipulation of the official accounts.

It was, however, his governing role at the Tower which permitted him to amass a fortune alleged to be as much as £50,000! The opportunity to harvest this vast sum arose because, the war being over but by no means forgotten, the State Prison held many former

Colonel Barkstead, Regicide

enemies, affluent Royalists who could be coerced into paying large sums of money to improve their confinement, for the provision of extra rations and the chance of exercise under escort within the walls. The relentless extortion continued unchallenged – for who dare defy one with such overwhelming authority – until 1659 when he was called to appear before the Committee of Grievances and account for his unscrupulous and avaricious actions.

Fearing the worst, Barkstead was galvanised into action. Such was the vigilance of the yeoman warders and soldiers on duty at the gates, that removal of his fortune from the precincts of the Tower was obviously out of the question; accordingly he packed his ill-gotten gains, doubtless comprising gold coins, into butter firkins, small barrels, and buried them 'in a cellar' within or near the Lieutenant's Lodgings (now known as the Queen's House) hoping that should the worst come to the worst, he could perhaps return to the Tower some day and retrieve the loot. His presentiments proved correct, for on 10 June that year he was severely reprimanded and, being dismissed from his post, he retired to his estate at Acton in Middlesex.

Less than a year later, in May 1660, Charles II, having been invited by the Convention and endorsed by popular opinion, to return as Sovereign, landed at Dover. At the prospect of the retribution which was bound to be directed towards those judges who had condemned the King's father to death, many of the regicides fled to the Continent, Barkstead settling at Hanau in Germany, where he became a burgess. But after some months, deeming himself out of reach of those who would exact their revenge, he became overconfident, and decided to visit friends across the border in the town of Delft in the United Provinces, Holland, together with two other regicides, Colonel Okey and Miles Corbet. While 'discussing affairs in England over a pot of Beer and a Pipe of Tobacco' in an alehouse in the Hooft Straet in that town, they were arrested and given into the custody of the English Resident, the 'ambassador'. This gentleman, George Downing, had been a high-ranking Republican but at the Restoration of the Monarchy conveniently abandoned his socialist principles and changed sides; now, without a qualm, knowing that certain death awaited his captives, one of whom, Colonel Okey, had actually been his commanding officer during the Civil War, he ordered the three to be shipped on the *"Blackamore"* to England, where ironically for Barkstead, they were imprisoned in the

WHILE STILL ALIVE AND CONSCIOUS—a victim's stomach is ripped open and his entrails burned in front of him.

A. Intestines are unwound from a man's stomach.
B. A man is buried alive.
C. Children being hewn to death.
D. A man has his stomach opened while still very much alive.

'Hanged, Drawn and Quartered'

Tower. While there, a woman calling herself Mary Barkstead petitioned the King that she might visit her husband, but permission was refused, and shortly afterwards the regicides were carried to Tyburn where they were publicly hanged, drawn and quartered. Even more ironically, after the disembowelling, Sir John Barkstead's head was displayed on a pike over Traitors' Gate!

But what of the treasure? Well, it appears that before fleeing to Germany, he had confided the approximate whereabouts of the buried gold to this 'Mary Barkstead' (although there is no record of his being married), and it was likely that her intention in visiting him in prison was to establish the exact location of the cache. Denied this opportunity and realising the impossibility of her gaining entrance to the Tower, let alone the Lieutenant's Lodgings, to retrieve the treasure, she subsequently took a certain Captain Evett into her confidence. This officer enlisted the assistance of a 'Mr Wade of Axe Yard', a friend of Lord Sandwich, to whom he passed on the information. His Lordship's secretary was none other than Samuel Pepys who, in October 1662, wrote in his Diary 'To my Lord Sandwich, who was in his chamber all alone, and did inform me that an old acquaintance hath discovered (disclosed) to him £7000 hid in the Tower, of which he has to have two for the discovery, my lord two and the King, the other three thousand, when it is found.' (Mary Barkstead was later to claim that the value of the treasure was £50,000, so one wonders whether the total had been deliberately understated by her, the Captain, Mr Wade or indeed all three, so that following recovery of the gold, only £7000 would be handed over to the Earl!). Pepys was also told that warrants would be issued authorising him and a Mr Lee, probably a clerk to the Council, to search the relevant premises, and after some little delay the search party, consisting of Pepys and Wade, Captain Evett, William Griffin (the door keeper at Pepys' office in Mincing Lane near Tower Hill), and a porter carrying the necessary picks and shovels, proceeded to the Tower where they obtained a candle, and started their search of the Lieutenant's Lodgings. It soon became evident that there were no cellars in that particular building; however, on passing through the communicating door leading into the adjoining Bell Tower, the hopes of the searchers must have revived on seeing that its lower chamber actually resembled a cellar, being a high arched vault with an earthen floor.

Later, Pepys wrote; 'after a great deal of council whether to set up on it now or delay for better or more full advice, we set to it, to digging we went to almost eight o'clock at night, but could find nothing. But, however, our guides Wade and Evett did not at all seem discouraged; for that they being confident that the money is there they look for, but having never been in the cellars, they could not be positive to the place, and therefore will inform themselves more fully now they have been there, of the party that do advise them. So locking the door after us, we left work to-night.' And having ensured that the Deputy Governor would 'undertake to keep the keys of the cellars and see that none go down without his privity' they all went home, Pepys not unnaturally, continuing to wonder what would be in it for him, a later entry in his Diary commenting 'If we get it, it may be I may be £10 or £20 the better of it.'

After dinner on 1 November, a Saturday, Pepys reported that he, Lee and Wade 'went with Captain Evitt and labourers, to the Tower cellars, to make one tryall more; where we staid two or three hours digging, and dug a great deal all under the arches, as it was now most confidently directed, and so seriously, and upon pretended good grounds, that I myself did truly expect to speed; but we missed of all; and so we went away the second time like fools.'

Disconsolately, Pepys, Wade and Evett adjourned to the nearby Dolphin Tavern where, over a flagon of ale, the Captain eventually and with much argument succeeded in persuading Pepys to continue the search, assuring him of the accuracy of the information he had been given, for it had come from Barkstead himself before fleeing the country. Somewhat convinced, Pepys arranged that two days later, being a Monday, they would meet at his office. There, the officer stated that not only had he consulted with his informant, a woman, over the weekend, but that if the search was resumed on the Wednesday, she, suitably disguised, would be present to assist in locating the spot. However there was a hitch in the arrangements and it was not until the 7 November that a third attempt was made 'and now privately the woman, Barkstead's great confident, is brought, who do positively say that this is the place which he did say the money was hid in, and where he and she did put up the £50,000 in butter firkins; and the very day that he went out of England did say that neither he nor his would be the better for that money and therefore wished that she and hers might. And so she left us, and we full of hope did resolve to dig all over the cellar, which by seven o'clock at night we performed. At noon we stopped and sent for a dinner, and upon the head of a barrel (not one of THE barrels! – Author) dined very merrily, then to work again. But at last we saw we were mistaken; and after digging the cellar quite through and removing the barrels from one side to the other, we were forced to pay our porters and give over our expectacions, though I do believe there must be money hid somewhere by him, or else he did delude this woman in hopes to oblige her to further serving him, which I am apt to believe.' One can almost sense their overwhelming feeling of disappointment after all their labours in that cold, dimly lighted vault.

However the lure of gold was still strong and a month later a final attempt was made, Evett averring this time that the treasure had been buried 'in the open garden before the Garden House' (i.e. that part of Tower Green fronting the Bloody Tower). But it was raining hard and the search was postponed until the following Friday, the 19.

On that day, Pepys and Lee, now getting thoroughly disillusioned, left the digging to the workmen and 'it being cold, we did sit all day till three o'clock by the fire in the Governor's house.' At that time they went out to inspect the progress but 'having wrought below the bottom of the foundation of the wall (probably of the Bloody Tower) I bid them give over, and so all our hopes ended; and so went home, taking Mr Lee with me, and after drunk a cup of wine he went away, and I to my office.......'

And so the treasure remained undiscovered. But were they looking in the correct place? Careful consideration would have convinced them that it would have been impossible for the Lieutenant to have dug holes and carried kegs to an open site such as the garden, or across to the cellars in any other building; the Tower was, and still is, virtually a village, with warders, members of their families and soldiers and servants constantly moving around. However, for what it's worth (£50,000?!), having lived in the Tower for a number of years, I have my own hypothesis as to where it still lies, based on the geography of the castle.

The inner and outer battlemented walls surrounding the Tower were for many centuries connected at intervals by cross-walls, like the spokes of a wheel, the defenders thereon being able to bring withering fire down upon any attackers who, having managed to bridge the moat and scale the outer wall, had dropped down into the casemates, the area betwixt the walls. To permit passage round the casemates, the cross-walls incorporated archways with heavy wooden gates and also small guard rooms manned only when danger threatened. And one such cross-wall bridged the area between the inner wall immediately adjacent to the north of the Bell Tower, and the outer wall.

The present route for the residents of the Queen's House wishing to leave the Tower is via Tower Green, the Bloody Tower archway and thence via the Byward Tower to the outside world. A much shorter route, especially when, in times of emergency or attack, the man commanding the castle had to get to the main entrance without delay, could have been from the Lieutenant's Lodgings via passages leading to a now non-existent doorway opening into the casemates adjoining, or perhaps even into, the small guard room of the cross wall situated there. If, as must be assumed, no trace was found after all Pepys' arduous labours in the Bell Tower itself, then where better

Lower Chamber of the Bell Tower

to dig a hole and secrete a fortune than beneath the floor of a deserted guard room? Alas, before readers seize their crowbars and spades and get into the ticket queue, I hasten to point out that that particular area is now a cobbled car park and is strictly out of bounds to the public! Moreover, if the treasure were found, what would be its true worth? What is the going rate for Commonwealth and Charles I coins? And would not so many hundreds of such coins flooding on to the collectors' market inevitably cause the price to depreciate? Nevertheless ....!

2. Roses for Anne Boleyn

'Because thou hast offended our Sovereign the King's Grace, in committing treason against his person, and here attainted of the same, the law of the realm is this; that thou shalt be burnt here within the Tower of London, on the Green, else to have thy head smitten off, as the King's pleasure shall be further known of the same'.

So ran the dread sentence of death passed on Queen Anne Boleyn at her trial, she having been found guilty of high treason by consorting with gentlemen of the Court, namely, Henry Norris, Mark Smeaton, Sir Francis Weston and William Brereton, and also committing incest with her own brother George. Spared the appalling fate of being burned to death, instead she was allowed the more merciful one of being decapitated by the sword. And because our traditional weapon of despatch was the axe, a French executioner from Calais (a town which at that time was an English possession) was sent for, wearing for the occasion a black, tight-fitting suit, a half-mask covering the upper part of his face, with a high, horn-shaped cap on his head. This fearsome looking uniform had been paid for by the Constable of the Tower, Sir William Knighton, Record Office accounts showing an entry of one hundred crowns in French money (£23.33 in English currency) 'to give to the executioner of Calays for his rewarde and apparail'.

The scaffold site had already been selected on Tower Green. 'Send at once to Master Eretage for carpenters to make a scaffold of such a height that all present may see it' ordered Sir William, and within days it was completed, five feet high, surrounded by a low rail and of course, its boards strewn with straw to soak up the corpse's copiously flowing blood.

At approximately six minutes past eight on the morning of 19 May 1536 Anne was escorted by two hundred Yeomen of the Guard to the Green and there, watched by nobles of the Court, aldermen of the City of London and officers of the Tower, she mounted the scaffold steps. After praying she allowed herself to be blindfolded, then knelt upright – no block was used with an execution by the sword, the headsman needing to swing the weapon horizontally – and he, picking the sword up from beneath the straw where he had compassionately hidden it, severed her head expertly with one blow. In duty bound, to demonstrate that the person condemned to death had indeed been executed, he then held her head high, it being reported that her eyes were still moving, her lips still framing her last prayer.

The scene that followed was graphically described by the historian Crispin who, two weeks later, wrote 'her ladies immediately took up her head and the body. They were so languid and extremely weak within anguish, but fearing that their mistress might be handled unworthily by inhuman men, they forced themselves to do this duty and at last carried off her deadly body wrapt in a white covering'.

The Tower authorities may have been efficient enough when it came to organising the building of the scaffold and the recruitment of the executioner – but where was the coffin? At length a yeoman warder used his initiative and procured an old arrow chest made of elm from the armoury nearby, into which the remains were reverently placed, and as it was too late in the day for the customary Mass to be said for the repose of her soul, her confessor Father Thilwall pronounced a blessing over the makeshift coffin as it lay in the Chapel Royal of St Peter ad Vincula.

Based on the obvious fact that the body remained in the Chapel for some time before being actually buried, rumours circulated over the next few months that her friends, the Wyatts, had secretly removed it from the Chapel and taken it to rest in Sale Church, near Aylesford in Norfolk,where many of her ancestors lie buried, this place of worship being situated close to Blickling Hall where she was born. Some accounts described an oak chest, heavily clamped with iron, in which her body was placed; others mention an unmarked black stone as being that which covered her grave. Centuries later, that stone was raised, nothing of note being found beneath it. Other gossip averred that her heart, in a casket, had been secretly buried in a church at Thetford, in Suffolk, but little credence should be given to such rumours.

In 1876 the remains of all those interred within the Chapel Royal were exhumed and decently reburied in the Crypt; among the remains beneath the altar were those attributed to Anne Boleyn, although there was no trace of the sixth finger or the third, rudimentary, breast she reportedly had.

Queen Anne Boleyn

The four alleged lovers, each found guilty of having carnal knowledge of the Queen, suffered similarly, all being executed. One, Mark Smeaton, a musician, succumbed to the dual persuasions of the torture instruments in the White Tower and the offer of a pardon, and confessed his guilt. However, the court reneged on him and, as he was a commoner, he was hanged, although not drawn and quartered.

Henry Norris, one of the grooms at Court and an erstwhile friend of the King's, incriminated by having picked up a handkerchief dropped by Anne at a tournament and then holding it to his lips, was imprisoned in the Martin Tower. Under interrogation, he said that he would rather die a thousand deaths 'than accuse the Queen of that which I believe her in my conscience innocent'. To which Henry VIII riposted 'Hang him up then!' That particular method however was not employed, for Norris, Sir Francis Weston and Brereton, being gentlemen, were all beheaded on Tower Hill two days before Anne met her death, witnesses describing how 'the executioner shed tears, but the bleeding corpses were allowed to lie for hours, half dressed.' Anne's brother George was accused of committing incest with Anne and brought to trial, his vindictive wife Lady Rochford testifying against him, but the only charge levelled was that having entered his sister's chamber one morning, and while conversing with her in the presence of her attendants, he had rested his hand on the bed. Incredible as it may seem, he was found guilty and duly beheaded. Retribution later overtook his widow, she in turn being beheaded at the same time as Queen Katherine Howard in 1542.

Mystery shrouds the exact burial place of the four men found guilty of being Anne's lovers. That they were all buried within the Tower is not disputed, and their freshly covered graves would have been seen by the luckless Queen as she approached the scaffold. Wriothesley's 'Chronicles' stated that 'Weston and Norys (were buried) in the churchyard of the same in one grave, Mr Bruton (Brereton) and Markes (Smeaton) in another grave of the same churchyard within the Tower of London'. The Tower's cemetery, like that of most churches, surrounded the Chapel and spread in a north-easterly direction, now the site of the Waterloo Block and Jewel House. When the foundations of that building were being prepared in 1841, a number of coffins and bones were unearthed and were re-interred in the Chapel's Crypt, as were other remains discovered in that area in 1964 and later.

Card accompanying the roses for
Anne Boleyn's grave

But the greatest mystery of the whole tragic episode is that of the anonymous tribute paid annually to the dead Queen's memory. Each year, stretching back at least since the early 1960s and doubtless originating long before that, roses are delivered to the Tower, sometimes in a basket, other times as a bunch, accompanied by a small card decorated with red roses and bearing the simple message 'Queen Anne Boleyn 1536'. And on the anniversary of her execution, 19 May, they are reverently laid on her gravestone before the altar and allowed to lie there until withered, then carefully removed.

Red roses are pictured on Anne Boleyn's coat of arms, grouped around a tree stump on which a bird is perched. A similar scene is also inscribed on one of the stone walls in the Beauchamp Tower, leading one to wonder whether one or more of the men accused of consorting with her, had been imprisoned in that particular cell.

The blooms are delivered by a renowned London store on the orders of an equally anonymous firm of trustees, but no serious attempt has ever been made to establish the identity of those initially responsible, in the belief that such wishes should be respected, and it is hoped that such will continue to be the case. Such heart-warming traditions should not be shattered in the mistaken and short-sighted belief that mysteries are simply there to be solved.

As an afterthought; in the light of the public's overwhelming expressions of grief at the sudden death of a twentieth century Royal personage, Diana, Princess of Wales in 1997 and the subsequent carpets of flowers which were laid as tributes around Buckingham Palace and Kensington Palace, one conjectures whether floral tributes similar to the 'Boleyn Roses' will appear on *her* grave four hundred years hence. One likes to think so.

3. *The Ghostly Hand at Traitors' Gate*

In December 1994 Shannon John, an attractive young American student, was one of a school group who came to this country to study Tudor history. In London they indulged in the inevitable round of sight-seeing, visiting such national institutions as the National Portrait Gallery, St Paul's Cathedral, the Bank of England and then like so many others, they came to the Tower of London. But when the list had earlier been compiled of places the group just had to see, little did Shannon and her family imagine in their wildest dreams that this was going to be an experience they had never expected – for only yards from the office blocks and speeding traffic of modern London, there, among the crowds of tourists on Tower Wharf, some-one from a bygone age was very, very close to Shannon!

I first became involved in the story when my colleague Yeoman Warder Brian Harrison, knowing of my research and subsequent books on the Tower's ghosts, forwarded a letter to me from Shannon's father, Mr Arthur D John of Redlands, California in which he enclosed a photograph of Traitors' Gate taken by his daughter and enquired whether we could account for the gloved hand which mysteriously appeared in the picture.

To say that I was intrigued is putting it mildly, for while I had on record many cases in which spectres had apparently appeared to people, ghostly sounds heard and even inexplicable odours, incense etc., smelled, this was the first occasion of which I was aware, of such a manifestation being reportedly captured on film! Caution of course was necessary that it was not a hoax, a technical malfunction, a double exposure or the like, and on discussing it by phone with Mr John I was reassured that it was indeed a bona fide request for enlightenment and not a stunt for publicity (if it were, it would have appeared in American newspapers and not queried at all with the Tower authorities, who would have simply dismissed it as such). A print of the picture providing few clues as to whether it was genuine or not, Mr John offered to send the original roll of film, as the negative concerned and those immediately adjoining it were of course essential for evaluation.

The ghostly hand at Traitors' Gate

On its receipt, I accepted the risk of being greeted with ribald scepticism and invited not only military photo-interpretation experts for an assessment, but later also the manufacturers of the film, they having the specialist equipment necessary to investigate the authenticity or otherwise of the negative. This they did thoroughly, over a lengthy period, and although they were necessarily wary of attributing the hand as being of supernatural origin, their conclusions can be summed up as follows;

1. 'The hand was not the result of a double exposure'.
   Comment: this was also confirmed by study of the other negatives on the roll.

2. 'Despite enlarging, then darkening the picture to varying degrees, the hand was still visible, surrounded by a strange glowing halo, especially round the thumb, this resembling the electro-fluorescent photographs interpreted by some as the 'aura' which surrounds us all, its colour signifying our mood e.g. blue for sadness, orange for happiness.' Also, as will be seen by the illustration, while the railings are out of focus, the end of the sleeve itself, the wrinkles in the material and the outline of the fingers are clearly delineated, yet both are the same distance from

the lens.

Comment: point taken.

3. 'The image of the hand was present in the scene when the photo was taken and had not been subsequently superimposed by computer or any other method.'

Comment: obviously an undisputed technical conclusion. Mr John also stressed that Shannon did not have the technical knowledge required to fake a picture in that way.

5. 'A hand could have intruded and been captured by the flash to give that luminescent effect, a known but rare phenomenon.'

Comment: Shannon said that there were only herself and a friend in the immediate area and she did not use the flash on her 'point and press' camera. Nor is the lacy Tudor or Stuart style cuff worn by the 'hand' the usual fashion adopted by touring students! Even had someone obtained a sleeve as a joke, the wearer would have instinctively curled their fingers round the railings in the picture. Close examination shows that this is not the case. If the hand is of an era long since gone, the fingers could not have curled round the railings anyway, because they weren't there, having only installed about a century ago to prevent people falling into the water below.

Several questions remain unanswered and are probably unanswerable anyway. The posture of the hand itself is unusually awkward, as attempts to curl the fingers in that manner, yet keep the thumb line straight, will demonstrate. Was the owner of the hand a man or a woman? Was he or she wearing a glove? – there appears to be wrinkles on the first finger and no thumb nail is visible. Was it a coincidence that the manifestation occurred where it did, at Traitors' Gate, the entrance through which the doomed victims were brought, to face lengthy incarceration or even death beneath the axe? It was certainly at the precise spot where, as I recounted in my book *Beefeaters of the Tower of London*, at 7.30a.m. on 11 March 1980 a passer-by witnessed and described in great detail a procession of Tudor-clad men and women, the men bearing pikes, the women resplendent in dresses studded with pearls and diamonds, one carrying a prayer book with a cross on it, the party passing slowly, as if in a barge, under Traitors' Gate and proceeding into the Tower. Had he seen a phantom re-enactment of the moments when Queen Katherine Howard, accompanied by four ladies and conveyed in a small boat rowed by four men, passed under Traitors' Gate on 10 February 1542, Katherine dying beneath the axe later on Tower Green? My informant reported that his attention was first attracted by a flickering haze of blue light beneath the archway; could it have been a glow similar to that which surrounded the 'hand'? So whose hand was it? We will never know. I have only one regret – that Miss Shannon John wasn't standing back sufficiently far enough to film whoever was on the 'other' end of the sleeve!

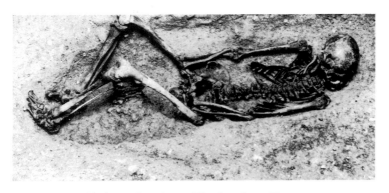

Skeleton found near The Lanthorn Tower

4. Skulls, Skeletons and Secret Tunnels

In addition to the many skulls buried in the Chapel Royal of St Peter ad Vincula, two others are visible in that place of worship. In the north wall of the chancel stands the Blount Memorial, the largest in the chapel. Constructed of alabaster and marble, it is actually a double memorial consisting of two matching halves commemorating the unique service rendered by a father and son who served as Lieutenants of the Tower during the reign of Queen Elizabeth I. The right hand half marks the tomb of Sir Richard Blount, Lieutenant of the Tower 1558-1564. He died 11 August 1564 and the monument was erected by order of his widow. On the Memorial he is represented as praying; behind him kneel his two sons, while Lady Blount and their two daughters kneel facing them.

The left hand section is that of Sir Michael Blount, who was appointed Lieutenant in 1588 and served for an unknown number of years. His effigy, also clad in armour, and those of his family, consisting of his wife, three sons and one daughter, were placed near that of his father thirty-two years later.

Above the alcoves, two skulls purporting to be those of the two Lieutenants, look down from circular niches. On examination some years ago, one proved to be genuine, though exactly of which Lieutenant, is not known; the other had been stolen sometime in the past and had been replaced by one made of alabaster. It is said that the latter material feels colder than does bone but that was not apparent to the author who, on reaching up one day and touching them, was unable to detect any difference! A skull is also carried by one of the kneeling females but would seem to be integral with the figure itself. It symbolises widowhood, as does the cap streamer thrown forward over the head of the other female effigy.

Other than in the Chapel, skeletons have also been found. In 1976 excavations were taking place in the Inner Ward, i.e. within the inner wall, south of the White Tower, where the steps near the souvenir shop lead up to the Lanthorn Tower. As usual in the Tower of London, the digging was done methodically and with great care, lest any fragile

Tomb of the Blount Family in St. Peter's Chapel.

artifacts be damaged before being seen and retrieved, but those engaged in the task could hardly have expected the sort of fragile artifact they DID uncover! The first indications of something out of the ordinary occurred when, at a depth of about fifteen feet, a pair of human knee caps appeared above the level of the soil. Work was immediately stopped and the experts summoned; trowels were discarded, to be replaced by brushes, and at long last, after careful and meticulous removal of the surrounding earth, an entire skeleton lay exposed!

As can be seen by the illustration, he lay in a grave too short for him, for his knees were bent as if he had been gently lowered into the cavity. His head was slumped to one side, to reveal a gaping hole in his skull but in all other respects his anatomy was complete and apparently undamaged. There were no primitive weapons or other items buried with him, nor traces of clothing of any sort. With great care he was removed and his bones later carbon-dated, the eventual conclusion being that he had lived in about the year A.D.70! He had been lying there, his presence unsuspected by the literally millions of people who had walked over his grave during the past one thousand nine hundred years. It was further concluded that, having been

25

buried within the old Roman Wall that encircled the City of London, the likelihood was that he was an Anglo-Saxon, for the Romans always buried their dead outside their city walls. At the Tower, history is literally under one's feet.

Also below ground were, and doubtless still are, secret passageways. In medieval times, when the Tower was a palace and court, prison and armoury, Mint and Record Office, it was home to, and workplace of a motley collection of aristocrats and high officials, warders and soldiers, servants and families, all crowded into what was, after all, a fairly limited area within the walls. In times of crisis, when political prisoners had to be transferred between various locations or in and out of the Tower, it was essential that this should be done surreptitiously to avoid comment or to ensure security. Should the government of the day not wish to bring prisoners in via Traitors' Gate and through the crowds milling under the Bloody Tower archway, they were able to bring them ashore at the Wharf and conduct them over the Middle Drawbridge into the Inner Ward, then via a tunnel leading directly into the underground chambers of the White Tower – where the torture instruments waited in readiness.

That there were tunnels running in that general direction is evidenced by the account of the imprisonment of one Thomas Sherwood who in November 1577 suffered 'in the dungeon among the rats', the earthen floor of which was below the high-water level of the River Thames. At high tide therefore, in the days when the uncontrolled river was much wider than it is now, the filthy waters would flood the tunnel, driving before it the hordes of scampering, squeaking rats which infested the river banks. In the darkness of the bitterly cold cell, the prisoners would not dare to relax but would need to repel the vicious onslaught as long as their strength held out, a contemporary report stating that 'flesh had been torn from the arms and legs of prisoners by these ferocious creatures'.

During excavations in the last century an underground passage was actually discovered leading to the White Tower. In later, more civilised days, it could have been the one which was utilised, not as a covert entrance for prisoners, but to convey bulky consignments of goods directly into the store -rooms of the White Tower, an easier route than attempting to carry them down the spiral stairways or through other apertures. More recently, in the 1970s, the southern end of such a tunnel was uncovered (and inspected by the author), but further exploration was unfortunately impossible as it had been backfilled.

Ways in which to escort prisoners clandestinely would also have been invaluable in other parts of the fortress. Many prisoners were interrogated in the Lieutenant's Lodgings (now the 'Queen's House') and, if failing to co-operate, were threatened with torture. If this did not have the desired effect, they were taken and first shown the rack and other persuasive instruments; if still not convinced of the need to tell all, torture in all its many varieties was applied. But how to take the prisoners from the Lieutenant's Lodgings to the torture chamber in the White Tower, with other prisoners under escort, residents, perhaps even the Lieutenant's guests strolling about Tower Green? Even more important, how to half-drag, half-carry the injured and semi-conscious victims back again, in full view of any passers-by? Moreover it may not have been expedient for the identities of the prisoners to become known. The solution was of course a tunnel running from the Lieutenant's Lodgings to the vaults of the White Tower. One of those who reportedly had to traverse it was John Gerard, a Jesuit who, in 1597, described how 'we went in a sort of procession, the attendants preceding us with lighted candles because the place was underground and very dark, especially about the entrance. It was a place of immense extent and in it were ranged divers sorts of racks and other instruments of torture. Some of these they displayed before me and told me I should have to taste them........................'

Other hidden routes were the passageways which honeycombed some of the immensely thick walls, one being that which communicated with the Bowyer Tower, mentioned elsewhere. Another was constructed in the wall of the Beauchamp Tower, a notorious prison for suspected conspirators, and was used to conceal government spies whose job it was to eavesdrop on conversations between the prisoners. Over the subsequent centuries the entrances to these tunnels and passages would been have blocked up and are now indistinguishable from their surroundings, but in the coming decades more holes will be dug, more walls repaired, more renovations carried out, all for purely practical reasons; but in so doing, who knows what may be found, what mysteries solved?

5. The Phantom of the Waterloo Block

It was 3 a.m. on a cold morning in September 1980 and the sentry patrolling along the front of the Waterloo Block suddenly had the feeling that he was being watched. His colleagues were fifty yards or more away, walking their beats, everywhere was in darkness save for a glimmer of light through the arrow slits of the White Tower opposite, the brightest lights of all being those shining out through the large windows in the upper halves of the double doors of the Waterloo Block itself, lights which clearly illuminated the entrance hall beyond. Being a member of a Guards Regiment, he was not given to reacting to unusual circumstances in any other way than that of a highly trained sentry; those on duty in the Tower, whether soldiers or yeoman warders, the latter all being ex-Warrant Officers or Sergeant Majors, could hardly be classed as being susceptible to nerves, and their role was to observe and investigate anything out of the ordinary, especially at night.

Reaching the extremity of his beat at the end of the long building, the soldier turned about, his sixth sense still sending out warning signals. His eyes probing the shadows, he suddenly found himself looking at the Waterloo Block doors - to see through the glass windows a shape outlined by the strong lights behind, a silhouette of a man crouching and watching him! For a moment the soldier froze, his hands gripping his rifle; he knew beyond the shadow of a doubt that those doors, indeed all the doors, both internal and external, were securely locked. A thief would hardly stand in a brightly lit hallway, yet how could a member of staff or even a tourist, have been inadvertently locked in? Before he could think up a rational explanation, the shape moved away, and at that the sentry acted in accordance with his instructions; using his radio he called out the guard, and also the Armouries warden responsible for night security. His sergeant and colleagues quickly arrived, together with the warden who unlocked the doors. Not surprisingly the sentry was more than reluctant to enter the building, but within minutes, the possibility of terrorism being an constant threat, the whole building was subjected to a minute and thorough search by the armed soldiers for any unauthorised person on the premises. All security devices were checked, all rooms searched, but nothing untoward was found. The sentry, questioned extensively by the Officer of the Guard, as was the routine, could not be diverted from his story and the incident was entered in the Report Book as inexplicable.

Equally inexplicable were the events which occurred on the upper floor of the Block, where flats occupied by yeoman warders, Jewel House members and their families were situated. Security being the top priority at all times, all the residents were required to lock outer doors behind them on entering or leaving the building at night, yet during 1979 and the following year, two yeoman warders described how, at different times in the night and sometimes as early as 7 a.m., loud knocking was heard at their 'front' doors, entrances which opened on to a long corridor. No matter how quickly they reached their front doors, no-one was ever there. That they were the activity of some practical joker was discounted, such childish practices not being indulged in by fellow warders, and anyway, there were only three or four families along that corridor so any miscreant could easily be identified. However, both yeoman warders reported that on several occasions, on opening their doors and looking along the corridor, the swing doors further along were seen to be swinging slightly, as if someone had just passed through them – yet on investigation all the doors beyond were found to be securely locked, as were those in the opposite direction. These incidents continued for some months and then, as mysteriously as they had started, the knocking suddenly ceased.

An even more baffling event occurred on 30 July 1980 involving another yeoman warder who occupied a flat on the second floor at the east end of the Waterloo Block. On leaving his apartment and closing the door, he suddenly heard a voice say "Oh - sorry!" and on turning, saw a man standing by the swing doors situated about six paces away. Next moment the man had moved away, passing through the aperture where one swing door had been propped open. It was mid-day, broad daylight in the corridor and members of staff not immediately recognised did pass through the building, so there was nothing unusual about the incident – why should there be? And then the warder thought again; where was the fellow going? Following the route the man had taken, he found what he had subconsciously expected – that every room leading off the spiral stairs at the end of the corridor, both up and down the stairway, were securely locked, mainy of them barred as well. When questioned, the description he gave was not of a ghostly, be-ruffed Tudor courtier or Cavalier dandy – but of a man who wore an ordinary looking suit and a wartime-type brown pointed trilby hat!

This incident gave rise to much speculation, following as it did, an occurrence two months or so earlier when, at 4.15 a.m. on the morning of 24 April 1980, two patrolling sentries saw what they described as 'a tall dark figure' at the east end of the Waterloo Block. They immediately gave chase, pursuing the figure down the stone steps leading to the Casemates, the area between the two encircling walls, but found no trace of an intruder. Another sentry had also heard suspicious noises at that time and so the guard was called out and a thorough search made of the area, but with no positive results.

To ascertain the possible significance of these occurrences, whether linked or not, we must go back to the seventeenth century. Prior to 1694, the year in which the Grand Storehouse was built there, most of that area was the cemetery of the Royal Chapel of St Peter ad Vincula which is situated immediately to the west. The Storehouse, an imposing three storied building, was a vast depository of weapons sufficient to arm 60,000 men, together with thousands of historic artifacts, banners, drums, arrays of bayonets and pistols; even the surviving instruments of torture were displayed there. But on Saturday 30 October 1841 a devastating fire broke out in a small tower immediately behind it, a conflagration which eventually enveloped the Storehouse itself despite all the efforts of the Tower's fire brigade and those of the City. Thousands of Londoners lined the edge of the moat to watch the pall of smoke, the flames leaping high into the air, the collapsing roof and walls, and when dawn came there was little to see other than smouldering ruins.

The site was cleared completely and in preparing the foundations for a new building on the site, the remains of many bodies, including, it is believed, those of the alleged lovers of Queen Anne Boleyn, were found. As mentioned in another chapter, more remains were discovered in later years, all being re-interred in the Crypt.

The new building was the present Waterloo Block which, when completed in 1845, was called the Waterloo Barracks, its main use being to house the Tower's garrison of soldiers; it also contains offices, store rooms and as previously mentioned, accommodation for members of staff. Currently of course the Jewel House is also situated therein.

The building being so comparatively recent, the spectral 'crouching figure' and the knocking on the doors – if indeed they were supernatural occurrences -could possibly be attributed to eternally wandering spirits of long-dead medieval corpses still mouldering beneath the foundations although they would have hardly appeared as the man wearing a war-time type pointed trilby! On the other hand, all the reported phenomena could conceivably have been caused by the latter apparition, and the vital clue in this connection is that there was a prisoner actually held in the Waterloo Block, as recently as the Second World War. He was a German spy, Josef Jakobs, who was confined in a room in the upper floor at the east end of the Block – the same floor and in close proximity to where the 'man in the trilby' was sighted!

Josef Jakobs was born 30 June 1898 and on enlisting in the German Army, rose to the rank of sergeant, attached to the Meteorological Branch. Selected as an espionage agent because of his knowledge of the English language, he was issued with the civilian clothing necessary to pass without suspicion in England, wireless transmitting equipment with which to communicate with his German base headquarters, and an identity card identifying him as James Rymer. He was given sufficient funds in English currency to enable him to pay for accommodation and purchase food and drink, and was also supplied with a bottle of brandy in the event of emergencies. For immediate sustenance on arrival, should that be necessary, he was given an item of food designed to evoke instant nostalgia – a traditional German sausage!

On the night of 31 January 1941, wearing a parachute, he boarded an aircraft which then took off and headed for southern England. Once over the estuary of the River Thames, the pilot navigated by following the course of the river as far as Gravesend and Greenhithe, then turned due north to drop his passenger over North Stifford, Essex. On descending, Jakobs, doubtless in trying to avoid dropping into the tree tops of a wood, made a heavy landing in a field nearby, breaking an ankle. Incapacitated, unable even to bury his parachute and flying kit with the small spade he carried, he was helpless to avoid capture by the Army personnel patrolling in the vicinity.

The chair on which the spy sat when executed – note missing rung torn away by bullets.

It being obvious from the equipment he carried that he was on a subversive mission, he was taken to Brixton Gaol where he received medical attention to his injured ankle. He was then interrogated by officers belonging to the counter-espionage branch and it soon became apparent that such was his loyalty and sense of patriotism, there was no question of him defecting and becoming a double agent. Seven months after his capture, on 4 August 1941, he faced a Court-Martial, and after hearing all the evidence, Jakobs was found guilty and sentenced to death.

He was taken to the Tower of London and, as stated above, was lodged in the Waterloo Block, guarded by soldiers of the Scots Guards. Early in the morning of 14 August 1941, he was escorted to the miniature rifle range which before its demolition stood only yards from the author's apartment in the Tower. There, seated in a chair (because of his injured ankle) he was executed by an eight man firing squad under the command of Major P D Waters M.C., five bullets piercing the circle of lint positioned over his heart. His body was taken to the Tower mortuary, a room situated in the outer wall of the east moat, beneath the approach road to Tower Bridge, where a post mortem was carried out, after which it was conveyed to St Mary's Roman Catholic Cemetery at Kensal Green and there, after the appropriate funeral service, interred in a common grave.

Was he – could he have been – the 'man in a trilby' seen by the yeoman warder? The fact that words were spoken did not necessarily preclude 'him' from being an apparition; phantoms are sometimes quite vocal; unmistakeable screams have on occasion been heard emanating late at night from the execution site on Tower Green, and ghostly moans have also been reported from other places over the years. Were the knocks on the doors his appeals for help in escaping his prison? Was he the 'crouching man' at the Waterloo Block door who, on seeing an 'enemy' soldier through the window, turned away and disappeared? Could he have been the 'tall dark figure' seen by the two sentries vanishing down the steps to the Casemates – the route which led to the site of the rifle range? And does his spirit frequent that area as well? In 1979 a poodle owned by a yeoman warder's family living opposite, took to staring at the place where the range once stood, barking and growling as if witnessing something only it could see. Whether the apparition was that of Josef Jakob or not, may he, a brave and loyal soldier who died for his country, find eternal peace.

6. The Curse of The Koh-i-Nur Diamond

The crown worn by the Queen Mother on state occasions is unusual, not only because it is the only one in the collection made of platinum, but also because it includes among its many gems the magnificent Koh-i-Nur, the oldest of the major diamonds. It therefore adorns a crown worn only by a woman, in the belief held by some that it would otherwise bring misfortune and possible death if set in a crown worn by a man. This might be regarded as mere superstition, but as its history unfolds, perhaps even the most sceptic may revise their opinion!

Originally found in the mines of Golconda in the Deccan, India, it first came to the notice of Westerners in 1526 when it was owned by Sultan Baber, founder of the Mogul Empire in Hindustan. At that time it was uncut and weighed a prodigious 800 carats, and was described 'as being as valuable as half the daily expense of the whole world'. It later came into the possession of Shah Jehan, the Emperor of Delhi, who engaged a Venetian, Ortensio Borgio, to cut it into a more desirable and attractive configuration. That gentleman's efforts failed so abysmally that he was fined £1000 and was more than lucky to escape with his life.

On Shah Jehan's death in 1666 it remained with his family until the Persian, Nadir Shah, invaded India and defeated the Mogul Emperor Mohammed Shah in 1739. The spoils of war included the Delhi treasury, variously estimated at between thirty million and sixty million pounds! But on checking its incredibly valuable contents Nadir found that the most important stone (at that time widely famed but nameless) was missing, and all his efforts to locate and acquire it were without result until eventually he was approached by a woman who offered, no doubt at a price, to betray the secret of the gem's whereabouts. She divulged the fact that it was concealed in Mohammed's turban 'which he never on any occasion laid aside'! As she was a member of Mohammed's harem, the implications of her master's retention of his headgear at all times will be left to the reader's imagination!

Initially baffled, Nadir eventually hit upon an ingenious way of gaining possession of the coveted prize. Having already seized the bulk of the Delhi treasures and concluded a treaty with the defeated Mogul Emperor, he had no pretext with which to resort to further violence, so he skilfully availed himself of a time-honoured Oriental custom seldom omitted by princes of equal rank on state occasions. At a grand ceremony held in Delhi a few days after the peace treaty had been signed, Nadir suddenly took the opportunity of asking Mohammed to exchange turbans as a token of reconciliation and in order to cement the friendship they had just sworn for each-other.

Taken completely aback by this sudden move and having had no time to think of a way out of his predicament, Mohammed realised he had been cornered by his wily rival and so conceded victory with as good a grace as possible. He had little option, for the Persian had taken off his own national sheepskin head-dress, glittering with costly gems, and then proceeded to don the one passed to him by the crestfallen Mogul who, nevertheless managed to maintain the proverbial imperturbability of Oriental potentates, evincing no sign of annoyance or even surprise; indeed so indifferent did he appear, that for a moment Nadir feared he had been misled by his informant. Concealing his impatience as best he could, as soon as the long drawn out ceremony was over, he hastily withdrew to his tent, took the turban off and carefully unfolded it – to discover with uninhibited delight the long -coveted gem! Holding it up to the light and observing that the stone ran up into a peak resembling those of the great snow-clad heights of the Himalayas, he exclaimed ecstatically 'Koh-i-Nur!', the 'Mountain of Light!'

But the gem proved to be far from a lucky charm, for Nadir was murdered in 1747, the Koh-i-Nur and many other of his jewels passing to his feeble son, Shah Roch. He in turn was overthrown by rivals but, despite being cruelly tortured, persisted with amazing tenacity to refuse to divulge the whereabouts of the gem. In the hopes that if treated generously, he would become more amenable and so divulge its hiding place, he was given the post of governor of the city of Meshd, but when his new appointment became known, Aga Mohammed, Chief of Kauin, who, like many others, lusted after the wonderful diamond, decided that it should be his. Under the pretext of visiting a sacred shrine at Meshd he and his men made the necessary pilgrimage and after performing their devotions at the shrine, threw off their disguises and occupied the city. In the palace Aga Mohammed demanded, under the threat of torture that the Koh-i-Nur be handed over, but Shah Rokh protested that he no longer had the gem. He was then subjected to extreme persuasion, being deprived of food and water, even being racked, torn with red-hot pincers and finally deprived of his sight, a practice prevalent at that time in Persia and Afghanistan. Still he remained obdurate, consenting only to part with some lesser stones. At that the merciless invader devised a truly diabolical method of persuasion. He ordered the blind victim's head be closely shaven and encircled with a 'diadem of paste', boiling oil then being poured into the receptacle so formed. But even the appalling agony of this torture only induced the Shah to hand over the remainder of the jewels – but not the Koh-i-Nur!

In 1751 the Afghan Ahmed Shah came to Shah Rokh's assistance, overthrowing and executing the barbaric Aga Mohammed. The blind and mutilated prince was restored to the throne but doubtless as a result of the injuries he had received, he died soon afterwards, but not before sealing the alliance by presenting his new ally with the fatal gem.

On the death of Ahmed Shah in 1793 it passed down the family, first to to Ahmed's Shah's son, Taimur Shah, and later to his son Shah Zaman. But the curse took its toll again, Zaman's brother Shah Shuja sending his men to intercept Zaman on the road to Kabul and carrying out his order to pierce his brother's eyes with a lancet. Stoic and obstinate, Zaman refused to reveal the whereabouts of the Koh-i-Nur and was imprisoned in a desert stronghold for many years, but the stone was eventually discovered by an official of the court who, noticing something sparkling in the cell wall, found that it was one of the sharp angles of the fabulous gem, it having worn through the loose plaster where Zaman had hidden it! Shah Jehan proudly wore at all state functions, but the almost monotonous chain of tragedies continued, for he too was dethroned, being blinded by '*his*' brother Shah Mahmud in turn and driven into exile in the Punjab - nevertheless still retaining the Koh-i-Nur!

His host, Runjit-Singh, the 'Lion of the Punjab', equally obsessed with possessing the famed diamond, concentrated his efforts on Shah-Shuja's consort, starving her and depriving her of all her belongings and personal jewellery. Hearing of the hardships inflicted on his wife, Shah Shuja eventually capitulated and, being granted a substantial pension, he relinquished the stone to his erstwhile oppressor.

Runjit had the diamond set in a bracelet which he, like Shah Jehan, also wore on all public occasions but, only too aware of its malevolent influence over former owners, it was reported that on his deathbed in 1839 'he having satisfied his covetousness in the enjoyment of its possession during his lifetime, vainly sought to break through the demands of fate and to avert ultimate destruction of his family by bequeathing it to the shrine of Jaganath (Juggernaut) for the good of his soul and the preservation of his dynasty.' But his successors could not bring themselves to give up the doom-laden treasure; such was its fateful attraction that any risk was worth taking, and so it was deposited with other national treasures in the jewel house in Lahore, India.

However, Runjit's last wish, if not actually carried out, at least came true, in that the terrible trail of unimaginable torture and blinding finally came to an end. Runjit's descendant, Rajah Dhulip-Singh, was recognised as ruler by the British Government. But the mutiny of two Sikh regiments in 1849 brought about the complete annexation of the Punjab, the civil authorities then taking control of the Lahore Treasure under the provisions that all the property of the state should be confiscated to that great trading corporation, the Honourable East India Company, to settle the debt owed by the Lahore Government and also to compensate for the cost involved in quelling the uprising. In addition it was stipulated that the Koh-i-Nur should be presented to Queen Victoria.

So this fabulous diamond was brought to England and shown to the public at the Great Exhibition of 1851, held in Hyde Park. Visitors must have wondered what all the fuss had been about, the stone having been so unskilfully treated by the Venetian and other cutters that it looked little better than an ordinary crystal. At that time it weighed slightly more than 186 carats and with a view to reshaping its dimensions to greater advantage, Messrs Costers of Amsterdam were engaged, they however admitting that such was the original damage, many difficulties were involved. The actual work was done in London rather than in the Dutch workshops, and the responsibility of cutting a diamond of such value and historic interest is well illustrated by an anecdote current at the time. While Mr Sebastian Garrard of the Crown Jewellers was superintending the re-cutting, many professors and other experts attended to watch the work in progress, the majority of them being of the opinion that the stone would split into pieces during the operation. Whilst there, they encountered the head of the firm, Mr Robert Garrard and asked 'What would you do supposing the Koh-i-Nur does fly to pieces?' Mr Garrard pondered for a brief moment, then replied 'Take my name-plate off the door and run!'

To the connoisseurs the result was disappointing. Not only had the gem been reduced to as little as 106 carats, but its appearance still left much to be admired. It was agreed by all, however, that it was, and still is, a most extraordinary stone and it is true to say that the Koh-i-Nur remains without a rival in respect of the horrific but also romantic incidents in its history. Whether recent suggestions made by those acting on behalf of the descendants of Dhulip-Singh that the rightful ownership of the gem might be contested, are actually followed up, it should remembered there is no evidence that the baleful power of the gem has altogether waned; furthermore, should anyone be foolhardy enough even to attempt to steal it from the Tower's Jewel House – I strongly suggest that the thief be a woman!

7. The Puzzle of The 'Princes in the Tower'

Actually there was only one prince, for when King Edward IV died suddenly at Westminster on 9 April 1483, his eldest son Edward, without announcement, proclamation or ceremony, immediately and automatically became King Edward V; 'The King is dead, long live the King' was, and is, the long-standing rule made to ensure royal continuity. So whoever murdered the two youngsters killed the King of England.

When his father died, young Edward's mother, Elizabeth Woodville, decided that she would take him and his younger brother Richard, Duke of York, straight to the Tower and there, once in safe surroundings, her eldest son by her first marriage being Constable of the Tower, no time would be wasted in preparing the boy for his coronation, planned for 4 May; once having had the barons swear fealty to their new king in Westminster Abbey, she could feel safe against any possible rivals. But Edward was at Ludlow, and so Elizabeth arranged that the boy's uncle, Earl Rivers, the governor of the Ludlow household, should escort him to London. For some reason there was a hold-up in their departure and it was not until 24 April that the royal party eventually started their journey.

They got as far as Stony Stratford, where they met Richard, Duke of Gloucester, the late King's surviving brother, who said that because he had had word of a conspiracy against Edward he would take over the escort and from then on would look after his nephew and assume the role of his advisor, taking the title of Protector. And as Gloucester was accompanied by a party of heavily armed men, Earl Rivers realised the futility of arguing, especially as Gloucester immediately accused him of plotting against his (Gloucester's) life.

When Queen Elizabeth heard the news she, fearing Gloucester's motives in thus seizing her son, reacted as any mother would; in the words of Sir Thomas More 'in gret fright and heuines, bewailing her childes ruin, her frendes mischance and her own infortune, damning the time that euer shee diswaded the gatheryng of power aboute the kinge, gate herselfe in all the haste possible with her yonger sonne and her five doughters oute of the Palyce of Westminster in whiche shee then laye, into the Sanctuarye, lodginge her selfe and her coumpanye there in the Abbottes place'. And there, in the comparative safety of the abbot's chamber in Westminster Abbey, she waited with dread for her long-time enemy's next move, which was not long in coming.

Gloucester and the young King reached London on 4 May, acclaimed by the City's Lord Mayor, councillors and populace, the Duke presenting his young charge to them as their King. At first being lodged in the Bishop of London's Palace near St Paul's, within a few days, Edward was transferred to the Tower of London, ostensibly to be prepared for his coronation, now rescheduled for 22 June 1483, and Queen Elizabeth had been induced by means of threats to surrender the little Duke of York into Gloucester's keeping, he saying that 'the King lacketh a playfelowye and needeth disporte and recreacion'. So young Richard joined his brother Edward in the Tower, a last account of them together being reported in the *Great Chronicle of London* that 'durying this mayris yere the childyr of Kyng Edward were seen shotyng and playyng in the Gardyn of the Towyr by sundry tymys'. And no-one saw them after that except their murderers.

Scandalous statements, doubtless inspired by those who stood to benefit the most, then started to circulate round the City that the late King had had a marriage contract with another woman prior to his marrying Elizabeth Woodville, this fact effectively nullifying that union on the grounds of adultery; therefore the two boys were illegitimate; therefore Richard, Duke of Gloucester, as the late King's brother, was the most eligible to succeed to the throne. Accordingly, feigning reluctance, he allowed himself to be persuaded and so proclaimed himself King and was crowned in Westminster Abbey on 6 July 1483, a reign which was to last only two years, for on 22 August 1485 he was slain at the Battle of Bosworth Field, and the victor, Henry VII, came to the throne.

Descriptions of how the two boys died vary in detail but contemporary historians, together with confessions in 1502 by two of the murderers, lend some credence to the accounts. It would seem that a Sir William Tyrell was sent by Richard III with a letter to the Constable of the Tower, Sir Robert Brackenbury, ordering him to hand over the Tower keys to the bearer for one night. Upon Sir Robert doing so, Tyrell directed Miles Forrest, one of the boys' attendants 'a fellowe fleshed in murther before time' together with

Princes in the Bloody Tower,
Tower of London.

The Princes in the Bloody Tower – A Victorian impression.

John Dighton 'a big brode square strong knave' as More described them, to smother them as they slept in the Bloody Tower (at that time known as the Garden Tower). So about midnight the two assassins crept in and 'bewrapped them and entangled them, keping down by force the fetherbed and pillowes hard unto their mouths, that within a while smored and stifled, theyr breath failing, thei gaue up to God their innocent soules'.

When Tyrell was informed of the boys' demise he ordered the bodies to be buried near the foot of the stairs and the place to be covered with stones; he then rode to Warwick and informed Richard III of the success of the plot. Richard, although pleased, directed that the bodies be reburied in a more appropriate spot, they being the 'kinges sonnes'. Obedient as ever, Tyrell ordered the Tower's priest to do just that and the man 'toke vp the bodyes again and secretely entered in such a place, as by the occasion of his deathe, whiche onely knew it, could neuer synce come to light'.

Although all those actively involved in the murders were granted a general pardon by Richard, none of them ultimately profited from their crimes. Miles Forrest died not long afterwards and his wife received a pension; Tyrell was appointed Governor of the town of Guisnes near Calais, and awarded lands in Wales but was arrested in 1502 on a charge of treason against Henry VII. He confessed his guilt in the boys' murder and was decapitated by the axe in public on Tower Hill. Shortly after Tyrell had mounted the scaffold, Dighton also confessed his role in the murders and he too faced an executioner, being hanged at Calais.

After Richard's death at Bosworth, Henry VII sought desperately to locate the corpses of the two boys, if only to disprove the ugly rumours that they had been still alive after the Battle of Bosworth and accusing him of having had them put to death rather than give up the throne; he also needed firm evidence in order to unmask pretenders masquerading as one or other of the boys, but all the searches proved totally unsuccessful and remained so for nearly two hundred years.

It was on 17 July 1674, during clearance work in removing remove extraneous buildings adjoining the south side of the White Tower began, that a discovery was made. The contemporary historian Sandford wrote at the time that the workmen 'digging down the stairs which led from the King's Lodgings in the White Tower to the Chapel, about ten foot in the ground, found the bones of two striplings in, as it seems, a wooden chest, which upon the survey were found proportionable to the ages of those two brothers, viz about thirteen and eleven years. The Skul of one being entire, the other broken, as were indeed many of the other bones, as was also the Chest, by the violence of the Labourers who not being sensible of what they had in hand, cast the rubbish, and by that means preserved all the bones. The circumstances from the Story were reported to the King and upon the presumption that these were the bones of the said Princes, His Majesty King Charles II was graciously pleased to command that the said Bones should be put into a Marble Urn and deposited among the Reliques of the Royal Family in the Chapel of King Henry VII in Westminster Abbey'.

A directive was later given to Sir Christopher Wren for 'A Marble Coffin for two princes', continuing 'These are to signifie his Maiesties pleasure that you provide a white Marble Coffin for the supposed bodyes of ye two Princes lately found in ye Tower of London and that you cause the same to be intered in Henry ye 7th Chappell in such convenient place as the Deane of Westminster shall appoynt. And this shall be your warrant, given under my hand this 18th day of February 1674/5'.

When the urn was completed, an inscription was added stating, in Latin; 'Here lies the remains of Edward V and Duke of York. These loving brothers, while imprisoned in the Tower of London, were foully smothered in their beds by the command of their faithless uncle and unlawful king, Richard. After about 196 years the bones of these dear ones were found in the soil at the foot of a deep fosse leading to the Chapel in the White Tower, and identified by the fullest evidence on July 17th, 1674. Our most gracious King, Charles II, taking compassion on their bitter fate, ordained this memorial to these most unhappy princes, AD 1678, in the 30th year of his reign.'

Over the decades the continued existence of 'unidentified' remains in the Abbey must have irked some authorities until eventually, after strong representations had been made to the Dean of Westminster and others, and with Royal assent, permission was granted for the bones to be scientifically examined with a view to establishing whether or not they were indeed the remains of the two Princes.

On Thursday 6 July 1933 the urn was opened in the presence of the Dean and other officials. It was found that the bones filled an oblong cavity within the urn and it was at once apparent that they belonged to two human beings for a fairly complete skull and a portion of another lay on the top. Many bones were found to be missing but this was accounted for by the fact that, as earlier reported, the bones were at first thrown away by the workmen and had subsequently to be recovered from a heap of spoil. Some finger bones were later reportedly given to the Ashmolean Museum, Oxford, but the authorities there were subsequently unable to find them!

Among the dust at the bottom of the urn were found three rusty nails which may have belonged to the original chest in which the bones had been buried. No portion of velvet, rag or any other material was found. The bones were carefully lifted out and placed on a nearby table, the public then being excluded from the chapel and every facility provided to enable Professor William Wright F.R.C.S., F.S.A., of the London Hospital Medical College, President of the Anatomical Society, aided by Lawrence E Tanner M.V.O., M.A., F.S.A., Keeper of the Muniments of the Abbey and Dr George Northcroft, ex President both of the British Society of Orthodontics and of the British Dental Association, to make a detailed anatomical examination, the purpose of which was to establish first, whether it could be assumed beyond reasonable doubt that the remains were those of the two princes, secondly, whether any evidence of murder existed, and finally to ascertain whether they were alive or dead at the time of Bosworth, i.e. were they killed during the reign of Richard III or Henry VII.

The examination itself was detailed and protracted, (a copy of the anatomical report is in my possession – Author), but ultimately the experts delivered their conclusions. In layman's language they concluded firstly that the bones were those of children differing some two or three years in age as judged by the length of certain bones. The condition of one particular bone belonging to one body made it possible to say with every confidence that it belonged to a child who had not yet attained the age of thirteen and this was confirmed by the configuration of certain other bones. The judgment of Dr Northcroft, the dental specialist, also corroborated that conclusion. But could that boy have been Edward? Well, it is a matter of record that on 2 November 1470 the Queen, Elizabeth Woodville, gave birth to a son, the future Edward V in the Abbot's House at Westminster, an entry in the Patent Rolls for 1472 giving a grant to the young prince from the Duchy of Cornwall estates 'from Michaelmas to 2nd November following, on which day he was born'. So he would have been about twelve and a half at the time of his death.

The date of birth of the younger prince is not precisely known except that, the Queen being at Shrewsbury in August 1473, an entry in the list of bailiffs elected annually in that town states 'This year the ducke of yorcke was borne in the blacke frears within the towne of Shrewsbery, the wche frears standethe under Sainct Marys churche in the sayde towne estwards', and this corresponds to Professor Wright's conclusion that the age of the younger child, estimated by bone length and state of teeth, to be about midway between the ages of nine and eleven. The Professor was also able to trace evidence of consanguinity, blood relationship, because of features of no small significance in the bones and jaws of the two children.

Understandably few traces of the method of death were found except in the case of Edward's skull, where the experts found an extensive stain reaching from just below the eye sockets to the angles of the lower jaw. It was of a distinctly blood-red colour above and a dirty brown colour below, and because of the fading away of the colour at its margins, was obviously of fluid origin, in other words, a blood stain. Its presence, together with the complete separation of the skull from the torso, lent support to the traditional account of the manner of death 'under feather bed and pillows, kept down by force hard unto their mouths'.

As it is almost beyond the bounds of credulity to accept that two other children of equivalent ages and sanguinity could also have been subjected to a violent death and surreptitiously buried in the Tower of London, for whatever reason, the conclusion must be that the remains were in fact those of King Edward V and Richard, Duke of York.

It follows from the above therefore that if these bones are really those of the princes – and Professor Wright concluded that not only is there nothing from a scientific point of view against it, and in fact that the evidence is 'definitely more conclusive than could, considering everything, have reasonably been expected', then it can be said with confidence that by no possibility could either, or both, have been still alive on the 22 August 1485, the date of Henry VII's accession to the throne – and so the murders must have been committed at the instigation of Richard III.

On 11 July, the examination having been concluded and many X-ray photographs taken, the inside of the urn was cleaned and the human bones, wrapped in white lawn, were replaced by the Dean;

45

first the bones of Richard, then the limb and body bones of Edward, and finally the bones of his skull, together with a statement written on parchment, recording what had been done. He then read part of the Burial Service and the urn was re-sealed.

Could it be that the spirits of the two Princes still haunt the Bloody Tower? According to the book *The Tower of London* written by Lord Ronald Sutherland-Gower in 1901, 'two small ghosts, hand in hand, clad in white nightgowns, were seen around the Bloody Tower in the last century' and during the First World War, when that building was the residence of Yeoman Warder Gurney and his family, their daughter Nellie went up to bed via the spiral stairs to her bedroom, the one in which the Princes were believed to have been murdered. On reaching the bedroom she opened the door and saw 'two boys in funny clothes' on her bed. Startled, she turned back to the stairs and called down to her parents, who came running up, only to find the room empty, but the father and mother said that the room felt eerie, with a cold chill about it. As to be expected, they took Nellie down to sleep in their room, Yeoman Warder Gurney searching the building thoroughly the next day before reporting it to the Resident Governor of the Tower.

The author has in his possession a clock case made from the old timbers of the Bloody Tower, acquired when the rafters were replaced in the 1970s. If only that timber could somehow recount the events it had witnessed throughout the centuries, the date of the princes' deaths and the identities of those who had murdered them would no longer be a much-debated mystery. Perhaps the questions could be settled once and for all, were the bones subjected to DNA analysis, but it is believed that permission to carry out this process has not been granted. Only in that way could final and absolute proof be forthcoming, but one query lingers on. The younger prince was not only Duke of York but was also Earl of Nottingham and Duke of Norfolk. And in the same month as Gloucester was crowned King, he bestowed honours on two of his closest friends. One of them, John, Lord Howard, became Duke of Norfolk and Duke of York, and the other friend, Lord William Berkeley, was made Earl of Nottingham. As these titles were already held by the young Prince Richard – how did the King know that they were by then vacant and available? Regrettably the truth may never be known.

8. The Duke who was drowned in Malmsy Wine – or was he?

George, Duke of Clarence, was proud and arrogant, and intensely resented the fact that his elder brother Edward was King, even though that monarch had given him a dukedom. In 1460 Edward met and defeated Henry VI's army at Northampton, assisted by the Earls of Salisbury and Warwick, but the latter nobleman, later quarrelling with Edward, plotted with the Duke of Clarence, who had become his son-in-law, to overthrow the King and in 1470 they had gained so much support that Edward fled to Holland and Henry VI regained the throne. However, assisted by foreign allies, Edward returned to England in the following year, met and slew the Earl of Warwick, won the Battle of Shrewsbury and on 21 May sent the displaced King Henry VI and his consort Queen Margaret to the Tower. And on the following day Henry VI was found murdered in the Wakefield Tower, as related elsewhere.

On that occasion Edward forgave his impetuous brother for trying to bring about his downfall, but George failed to heed the warning. Not only begrudging his brother's success in life, he also openly displayed his dislike for Edward's consort, Queen Elizabeth Woodville; moreover he was foolhardy enough to try his luck once again in persuading those in opposition to the King to rise against him. Enough was enough; in June 1477 Edward summoned him to Westminster, charged him with treachery and conspiracy, and consigned him to the Tower. There George was confined for seven months, during which time Edward must have looked for some sign of contrition, some indication of penitence – the headstrong, stubborn Duke was after all his brother. But it was to no avail, and in January 1478 Parliament condemned the Duke of Clarence to death. And on 18 February, within the Tower of London, he paid the price for his treachery.

Strangely enough, so far as is known, the instrument of his demise was not the axe, to which he was entitled by rank and title, but a sweet Madeira wine, Malvoisie wine, 'rich, heady Malmsy'. Theories abounded about exactly what happened that night, and in view of the plots and counter-plots, the machinations of competing rivals at Court at that time, most are feasible if not factual. That Malmsy wine was involved, there seems little doubt, but did George, realising that the game was up, request a butt of his favourite beverage and have a final and fatal drinking session, consume a liquid overdose? Or did he defiantly seek that particular way out on purpose in order to cheat the executioner? Certainly, when found, he was slumped against the barrel, his head hanging over the side, although a more generous interpretation suggested that it could have been an accident; that having drunk his fill he had succumbed to the pungent fumes from the newly broached butt.

There were others who theorised that, far from it being suicide, the Duke had been murdered by first being poisoned and then immersed to make it appear an accident; yet others speculated that he had been forcibly drowned in the barrel, held struggling frantically under the surface until the bubbles ceased to rise. On the other hand, a few, a very few, discounted all these as wild rumours spread by malcontents and declared that nothing untoward had happened; the Duke had been executed by the axe according to the law and his decapitated corpse had been removed from the Tower in the wine barrel – although they could give no reasons for this mode of transport.

But who could have murdered him? It was common knowledge that his other brother, Richard, Duke of Gloucester, younger by three years, had been at odds with George for some years and he himself had ambitions to succeed to the throne, an ambition he was to realise five years later. Whether or not he was directly implicated, his enemies at Court were quick to accuse him of removing one who impeded that ambition, even though that meant killing his own brother.

The Duke had been imprisoned in the Bowyer Tower, a small bastion of evil reputation situated on the north side of the inner ballium wall. If murder had been the cause of death, those guarding the thick wooden door of the cell need never have known about the tragedy being enacted in the stone chamber behind them. No ill-intentioned group of men need have demanded admittance by that entrance, for the early architects of the castle incorporated ways of entering many rooms other than by the doors. Having been originally designed to defend the royal residents and its treasures, attacks on the Tower of London could be repelled by the garrison troops manning the battlemented walls moving rapidly from one point to another by passing through the upper stories of smaller towers, they being at the same level as the top of the walls, rather than having to descend to ground level and climb up again each time.

Similarly many of the eight -foot thick inner walls themselves were, and are, honeycombed with narrow passages fulfilling not only that purpose but others of more sinister intent. One of these passages, leading from the direction of the Flint and Devereux Towers, communicated directly with a vault beneath the Bowyer, and in the 1970s, the author was present when a paving stone in the ground floor chamber was raised, to reveal a flight of stone steps leading downwards, regrettably back-filled long ago. It would therefore have been a simple matter for those embroiled in a murderous plan, to enter the cell and overpower the Duke, drown him in the wine, then prop him against the barrel and depart, leaving behind no trace of their presence.

Whatever the method, Parliament officially accepted that George, Duke of Clarence had been legally executed in accordance with the sentence passed upon him. His remains were taken to Tewkesbury and buried with appropriate ceremony and here the matter ended – but the mystery will always remain.

9. The Decapitated Nun

The Tower of London is notorious chiefly for the three queens and a countess who, after being imprisoned there, were beheaded. It should not be forgotten however that another female prisoner of the Tower was also beheaded, albeit at Tyburn. This was in an age when women condemned to death for major crimes such as high treason were not hanged, drawn and quartered as were their male counterparts, because it was considered indelicate to dismember a woman in public; instead they were burnt to death, and in fact the death sentence passed on Anne Boleyn decreed that she was 'to be burnt alive or beheaded, at the King's pleasure'. Yet in 1534 a woman named Elizabeth Barton was decapitated on the orders of Henry VIII, becoming the only female whose head was displayed on London Bridge.

Elizabeth was born about the year 1506 and by the age of nineteen she was employed as a maidservant by a family living in Aldington in Kent. Contracting some epileptic-type disease which affected her brain, she became neurotic and prone to trances, and on recovery she would then describe the marvels she had witnessed while in that state. In an age of belief in witches, spells and sorcery, she soon became known locally as having the power of second sight, thereby attracting the attention of Edward Bocking and Richard Dering, two monks of Christ's Church, Canterbury, together with Henry Gold, Rector of St Mary Aldermary, Friar Rigby and Hugh Rich, Warden to the Observants at Canterbury. Bocking subtly influenced the young woman to direct her dire prophesies against opponents of the Roman Catholic Church and as word of her 'Divine Gift' spread throughout the country, learned men flocked to Kent to hear her prognostications. It is even said that Sir Thomas More and William Fisher, Bishop of Rochester, were inspired by her religious fervour, the latter ecclesiastic arranging for her to be admitted into the Benedictine Nunnery of St Sepulchre at Canterbury in 1527, where a cell was assigned to her.

Now being known as the 'Holy Maid of Kent', and doubtless believing all she experienced during her visions, her preaching

Severed heads on London Bridge

continued unabated, reaching its vehement peak when Henry VIII divorced Katherine of Aragon; incensed by blatant flouting of everything she considered holy, she prophesied that he would die within a month of marrying Anne Boleyn, adding fuel to the flames by declaring that he was no longer king in the sight of God and would die a villain's death.

Religious mania could be tolerated, just; high treason could not. In June 1533 she and her priestly supporters were arrested and brought to the Tower. There, sufficient pressure was brought to bear on her mentors by means of the usual Tower implements of torture and, their resistance crumbling, they admitted that the Maid was an impostor. She, on the other hand, blamed them, pleading that she was but a poor woman led astray 'by these men who should have known better, being learned clerics'.

In order to publicise these revelations, on 23 November of that year they were all taken to undergo a public penance at St Paul's Cross where 'there was as great a crowd as was seen there this forty summers'. From there she and the priests were, accordingly to the *Grey Friars Chronicle* 'returned unto the Tower and there were much people thro' all the streets to see her pass'. Back in the State prison she was imprisoned in the now long-demolished Coldharbour Tower near the White Tower, her cell becoming known as the 'Nun's Bower'.

In January 1534 Parliament met and in order to crush any further Catholic support for the alleged conspiracy, Elizabeth Barton and the others were condemned to death. The months dragged by until 20 April 1534, Wriothesley in *Wriothesley's Chronicles* reporting that they were all 'drawne from the Tower to Tiborn and there hanged, and after cutte downe and their heads smitten of, two of their heades were set on London Bridge and the other four at Diverse gates of the citee'.

The decapitations were in all probability carried out by one Cratwell, a public executioner noted for his cruelty, the Lord Chancellor describing him as 'a conninge butcher in the quarteringe of men'. Appropriately enough, four years later, he too met his end in a similar fashion, being 'hanged at the wrestling place on the backsyde of Clerkenwel besyde London, for robbing of a bouthe in Bartholomew's Fayre, at which execution was above 20,000 people attending'.

After the executions all the heads were parboiled, immersed in buckets of scalding water and a mixture of salt and cumin seed in order to deter the seabirds for as long as possible, and displayed as ordered by the court. Elizabeth's head was spiked on the Drawbridge Gate of London Bridge which, being the only direct route to and from the south, thereby ensured that the Maid's head, with its long grizzled black locks falling over its pallid features, would warn all Kentish folk of the dire consequences of invoking the King's wrath.

The reason why Henry VIII should have had the nun publicly decapitated and her head so displayed, when the hanging itself, followed perhaps by the corpse being suspended from a gibbet, would have been sufficient as a deterrent, is a mystery. There was certainly little or no precedent for such an abhorrent act at the scaffold as that, and leads one to wonder whether her decapitation, albeit after being hanged, gave him the idea of despatching two of his erring queens in a similar manner, a few years later, but unlike Elizabeth Barton, without first being strangled by the rope.

10. The Riddle of the Ravens

What could be a more appropriate collective noun for these large black birds than 'an unkindness of ravens', for they are not only markedly belligerent by nature but are also harbingers of doom, birds of ill omen, being endowed with a sixth sense of approaching death – not to themselves but to members of the human race. Throughout history the arrival of a raven at a dwelling has heralded the demise of the occupant, even though that person was apparently alive and well. The orator and statesman, Cicero (106-43 B.C.) was reputedly forewarned of his death by the fluttering of ravens, one of the birds entering his room and pulling the clothes off his bed on the very day he was murdered by Antony's soldiers.

In 1651 The philosopher Ross said "by ravens both publick and private calamities and death have been portended. Private men have been forewarned of their death by ravens; a young gentleman, Mr Draper, my intimate friend, who about five or six years ago (1646) being then in the flower of his age, had on a sudden, one or two ravens in his chamber, which had been quarrelling on top of the chimney; these they apprehended as messengers of his death, and so they were, for he died shortly afterwards". And Hall, in his *Characters* wrote in 1608 'if a superstitious man hears a raven croak from the next roof, he wastes no time in making his will'. The connection between the croak of a raven and the slang word for death may be purely fortuitous!

Ravens have lived in the City since time immemorial, inhabiting the steeples in the City's ancient churches and other high buildings, gorging themselves on the crusts of food thrown into the squalid streets, the raw meat scraps in the shambles of Smithfield market. And although their descendants are now housed, fed and protected in the Tower, in some mysterious way they still retain their age-old faculty of sensing death. It is said that when ravens forsake their normal abode, we may expect famine and mortality, and in the Tower the latter certainly applied, even to the extent of the birds leaving their own territory around Tower Green and the White Tower, to hop into the Casemates, the area between the inner and outer walls.

In instances related by Mr G D Trott, son of the Curator of the Jewel House (1921 - 1951) who lived in the Tower during most of those years, he tells how;

'One of the yeoman warders who lived in Legge's Mount (a tower on the northwest corner of the outer wall) was taken ill and just before he died a raven came down from the Green via the Flint Tower steps (see map) and went up the steps by Legge's Mount on to the battlements, where it started croaking. The Yeoman Ravenmaster went up to move him, but no luck. After the yeoman warder had passed away, the raven was seen to come down the steps and go back up the Flint Tower steps to the Green.

Another similar incident occurred near the Salt Tower. One night a sentry shot himself in the toilet nearby. When they found him early in the morning, a raven was croaking only a few yards away. The yeoman warders and their families who lived in the Well Tower and the Cradle Tower heard the noise, and after the body was taken away, the raven went back to the Green.'

Mr Trott also referred to the rifle range which used to stand in the Casemates between the Martin and Constable Tower and served as an execution shed in which firing squads despatched enemy spies in both World Wars. He described how; 'when the spy was shot in WWII my father and some of the yeoman warders saw him and the escort party come marching along the Casemates and just before they went into the rifle range, a raven had come down the steps by the Martin Tower and was croaking by Brass Mount. The senior officer tried to get rid of him but the warders said leave him alone! After the body was taken away to the Tower morgue in the moat wall by Tower Bridge approach, the raven went back up the steps again.'

In October 1950 Mr Trott's mother became seriously ill and he, together with warders and their wives, heard a raven croaking on the battlements above their apartment. 'Leave him, he will soon go' said Mr Trott's father, a prophesy which sadly came true.

One final excerpt from that gentleman's letter reveals the escapades he and others got up to in those blissful days of minimum security. 'If any soldier and sometimes us boys came in late and did not have our names in the book on going out (a requirement if intending to return late) or returning after 3a.m. (when readmittance was refused), we would get into the gardens from Tower Hill, drop down on to the rubbish dump in the moat and climb up a drainpipe to the east of the North Bastion on to the roof, then down the steps into the Casemates and away. One night a soldier did this and he fell off the pipe, injuring himself and later died. In the early hours when they found him, a raven had got on to the battlements and was croaking but it stopped when they found the soldier and hopped back to the Green'.

The mystery is, how do the ravens know? It is said that they are born mimics and can be taught to speak - but will they ever divulge the secret of their prophetic knowledge?

11. The Woman who was Racked

There could not have been a worse era in which to defy the law than when Henry VIII – and the rack – ruled! Many men writhed in agony as the levers turned, each click of the cogs bringing more suffering, more excruciating pain, yet only one woman was ever led into the vaults of the White Tower to be strapped to its unyielding frame, her wrists and ankles bound by the ropes which would pull her very joints asunder. Her name was Anne Askew.

Anne was the second daughter of Sir William Askew, or Ascough, of South Kelsey in Lincolnshire, and when she was fifteen she married Thomas Kyme of Lincoln, eventually bearing him two children. Thomas was a devout Roman Catholic, his faith leading to marked differences of opinion between them, for Anne, an outspoken woman at best, had decidedly heretical leanings, and supported the Protestant faith with vigour and total indiscretion, a dangerous combination in those perilous days. She became involved with others of like mind, and once admitted to their circle, found that the Queen herself, Katherine Parr, was not only sympathetic to their cause but spent much time discoursing at length with Anne and her fellow believers. It became even more dangerous to hold such Protestant beliefs when, in 1539, an Act known as the 'Six Articles' was passed, for the first clause stated that anyone who did not agree that the 'Natural Blood and Body of Christ were present during the Sacrament' i.e. one of the basic tenets of the Roman Catholic belief, would suffer death by fire.

Queen Katherine had long been the target of intense intrigue in Court and those seeking her downfall were quick to seize their opportunity. Accordingly they reported Anne to the authorities, hoping that it would also eventually lead to the Queen herself being incriminated. In March 1545 Anne was summoned to the Guildhall and after being questioned at length by Bishop Bonner, was allowed to go after having been cautioned as to her future conduct.

It would seem, however, that she disregarded the warning and three months later she was arrested and taken before Baron

Torture by the Rack in the Tower of London.

Wriothesley, the Lord Chancellor, and the Privy Council. Again she refused to abandon her own firmly held principles, and so was committed to Newgate Prison pending further interrogation at the Guildhall. There, once again, she held firm to her beliefs, despite being threatened that unless she renounced her errors, she risked being put to death. But even this did not deter her. Upon defying the Council to do their worst, she was then, without trial or jury, condemned to be burnt to death as a heretic. And instead of being taken back to Newgate, she found herself passing under the forbidding portals of the Tower of London – before facing the blazing pyre, the identities of her fellow believers HAD to be wrung out of her.

Meanwhile the Queen's enemies attacked on another front, Wriothesley using Anne Askew's blatant defiance and known friendship with Katherine Parr to draw up a Warrant for the Queen's arrest. Luckily for Her Majesty – otherwise three wives of Henry VIII would probably have been beheaded on Tower Green – the Lord Chancellor dropped the important piece of paper in a corridor of Westminster Palace, where it was picked up by one of the Queen's attendants. On realising the awful significance of the words, she hastened with it to her mistress who, not unnaturally, was horrified at its import. Immediately she sought audience with Henry who, again fortunately for her, was very ill and so susceptible to a little wifely cajolery. Showing every sympathy for his parlous condition, she managed to coax him into a forgiving mood, only just in time, for shortly afterwards the Lord Chancellor, now armed with a fresh warrant and accompanied by a number of soldiers, appeared in the Presence Chamber, only to receive the Tudor equivalent of a flea in his ear, Henry delivering a volley of abuse and threats. Whereupon the Baron 'was fain to retire, sorely discomforted and more than a little alarmed as to what might happen to him, and thus the matter ended'.

This royal rebuff obviously made Wriothesley determined to extract damning information in one way or another from the woman now in the Tower. Taken to the torture chamber she was first given the opportunity to recant and confess by being shown the rack. Her obstinacy being only too evident, the yeoman warders were then ordered to secure her to the frame, which they did so, binding the pulley ropes about her wrists and ankles. Present were Baron Wriothesley, Sir Richard Rich (who, only a few years previously, had perjured himself in order to ensure the downfall and execution of Sir Thomas More), Sir John Barker and the Lieutenant of the Tower, Sir Anthony Knivett. The questions came, but when Anne refused to name names, Wriothesley ordered the warders to turn the levers and so force her to confess.

The Lieutenant initially assumed, understandably, that at the first hint of pain, Anne Askew would tell all she knew. But at her continued silence, the prospect of further savagery being inflicted on her, shocked him so much that he protested vehemently and ordered his warders to stop; whereupon Wriothesley himself, incensed by the woman's obduracy, seized a lever and and pulled, increasing the tension on his victim's agonisingly extended limbs. Realising further appeals for clemency would be wasted, the Lieutenant then left the chamber, saying that he would report the outrage to the King himself. Wriothesley, having already been thwarted once because others had got to the King first, was determined not to let it happen again; releasing the lever, he strode out and, calling for his horse, mounted it and galloped off towards Westminster. But the wily Lieutenant, knowing the slow progress of a horseman through the City's narrow muddy streets, smartly outflanked the Lord Chancellor by boarding his own official barge which was anchored at Tower Wharf. The tide being favourable, within minutes the vessel was heading upriver, and as soon as it was moored by Westminster pier, Sir Anthony hurried to the King, to whom he recounted the events taking place at the Tower, the horrific torture to which the woman was being subjected.

Henry, disturbed by the lurid picture painted by the Lieutenant, instantly ordered the officer to return to the Tower and release the victim from the rack. Wasting no time the officer obeyed. Returning to the dungeon he summoned the Tower surgeon and together they revived the woman who, according to some, was 'fainting and half-crippled'. Over the centuries the degree of her suffering has always posed a mystery, many authorities affirming that it was indeed severe, basing it on Anne's own testimony quoted in Foxe's *Book of Martyrs* in which she said 'they did put me on the rack because I confessed no ladies or gentlemen to be of my opinion, and therefore kept me a long time on it and because I lay still and did not cry out, my Lord Chancellor and Master Rich took pains to rack me with their own hands, till I was nigh dead'.

Others, namely John Bale, Bishop of Ossory, stated in a work published in 1547 that she was able to discuss religious matters with her inquisitors for more than an hour after her ordeal, sitting on the edge of the rack. There was also a report that after being taken back to Newgate she 'sat talking pleasantly on godly things until very late' with her companions. Yet to be racked by the warders and then further by the Lord Chancellor, no matter how comparatively 'slight', must have physically disabled her to a much greater extent than that, for when she taken to Smithfield to be executed, she was too weak to walk and had to be carried in a chair. She might have been spared the torture of the rack by Royal command, but nevertheless she was still a heretic and so had to be burned alive.

At the place of execution she faced her persecutors, Lord Wriothesley and Sir Richard Rich who, together with the Lord Mayor of London, the Duke of Norfolk and Lord Russell, sat on a specially raised platform. After a sermon, Anne, dressed in white, was tied to a stake surrounded by heaps of faggots and brushwood. An enormous crowd of men, women and children surged around the scaffold, while others leant from windows and balconies, some even clinging precariously to the chimneys on the roof tops. Just before the executioner ignited the tinder-dry wood with a flaming brand, the Duke of Norfolk and the Lord Mayor, 'being considerably perturbed by a rumour that there was an unusual amount of gunpowder on the spot, manifested some alarm about their own safety! They were comforted by Lord Russell's assurance that there were only a number of small bags of powder concealed about Anne's person, to shorten her torments and speed her demise, but so disposed as to be harmless to the spectators!' The flames spread, the overwhelming heat causing the victim to writhe agonisingly in her bonds until, mercifully, the gunpowder exploded and killed her. And within a short time the body of Anne Askew, a martyr who held on to her principles to the very end, was consumed by the flames and finally reduced to ashes.

But the questions refuse to be so swiftly dealt with. Although being racked at all was almost unimaginable, how severely WAS she racked? And who, among the Queen's enemies, contrived to bring about such a torture never previously inflicted on a woman? Why did Henry VIII, having had no qualms about having two of his wives beheaded on Tower Green, act so out of character as to refuse to sign the arrest warrant in respect of Katherine Parr? And not being known to show mercy towards heretics, why did he refuse to allow the continued torture of Anne Askew? Was it because the use of the rack was regarded with such horror by the population that it was the standard practice to apply it in secret, a secret which, should it be exposed by the possible death of Anne under torture, could have resulted in an uncontrollable public outcry - and make the further use of the instrument untenable?

12. Was Colonel Blood Paid to Steal the Crown Jewels?

Admittance to the Tower by the general public is not a recent innovation but originated in the seventeenth century, one of the first visitors being a Colonel Thomas Blood who was caught in the act of trying to steal the Crown Jewels – but far from being tried and punished, in those days when the theft of only a handkerchief brought sentence of death, he was actually rewarded, for reasons which were never divulged.

This attempted armed robbery would never have happened had it not been for the fact that Sir Gilbert Talbot had recently been appointed Master and Treasurer of the Jewel House, the Regalia at that time being displayed in the Martin Tower at the north-east corner of the Inner Ward. The emoluments, the income that went with the post, had been severely reduced but to compensate for that, King Charles tacitly allowed him to exhibit the Jewels to members of the public, and charge a fee for the privilege. Understandably, a knight of the realm could hardly be expected to perform a task as menial as mixing with the general public of the day and so he delegated the job to an elderly gentleman named Talbot Edwards, who had been servant to Sir Gilbert's father. Edwards and his family were then allowed to 'live over the shop' by moving into the upper rooms of the Martin Tower, quarters which had their own separate entrance and Edwards was doubtless permitted to keep a small percentage of the admission fees as his wages.

It was early in 1671 that Thomas Blood, a man then aged about fifty, entered the scene and who would play a leading role in the drama which would unfold during the weeks to come. He was an Irishman who had joined the Commonwealth army and attained the rank of colonel, and was described as a man of great energy but of ruffianly character. In April of that year he visited the Tower disguised as a man of the cloth, a parson, and was accompanied by a woman he introduced as his wife. What happened next was related later by Talbot Edwards to the historian John Strype (1643-1737) who in 1720 included the account in his reprint of Stowe's *Survey of London*. To recapture the atmosphere of those times it is recounted here in the style he used.

'They desired to see the Regalia and just as their wishes had been gratified, the lady feigned a sudden disposition, a qualm on her stomach; this called forth the kind offices of Mrs Edwards, who having kindly invited them into the house (apartment) to repose herself, she soon recovered, and on their departure they professed themselves thankful for this civility. A few days after, Blood came again, bringing a present of four pairs of gloves from his pretended wife, and having thus begun the acquaintance, they made several visits to improve it. After a short respite of their compliments (visits) the disguised ruffian returned again and, in conversation with Mrs Edwards, said that his wife could discourse of nothing else but the kindness of those good people at the Tower, that she had long studied and at length bethought of a handsome way of requital. 'You have' quoth he 'a pretty young gentlewoman for your daughter, and I have a young nephew who has two or three hundred a year in land, and is at my disposal. If your daughter be free, and you approve it, I will bring him here to see her, and we will endeavour to make it a match.'

This was easily assented to by old Mr Edwards, who invited the pretended parson to dine with him on that day; he readily accepted the invitation, and taking upon himself to say grace, performed it with great seeming devotion, and casting up his eyes, concluded it with a prayer for the king, queen and royal family. After dinner he observed a handsome case of pistols in one of the rooms and expressed a great desire to buy them, to present to a young lord who was his neighbour; a pretence by which he thought of disarming the house against his plan to steal the Jewels. At his departure he appointed a day and hour to bring his young nephew to see the daughter; which was the very day on which he made his daring attempt.

The good old gentleman, Mr Edwards, had got up at seven in the morning ready to receive his guest and the daughter was in her best dress to entertain her expected lover, when behold, Parson Blood, with three more men, came to the Jewel House, all armed with rapier blades hidden in their canes, and every one a dagger, and a brace of pocket pistols. Two of his companions entered with him on pretence of seeing the crown and the third stayed at the door, as if to look after the young lady, but in reality, as a lookout. The daughter, who

COLL. BLOOD

Colonel Blood.

thought it not modest to come down until she was called, sent a maid to take a view of the company and bring a description of her gallant; and the servant, conceiving that he was the young intended bridegroom who stayed at the door, being the youngest of the party, returned to soothe the anxiety of her young mistress with the idea she had formed of his person.

Blood told Mr Edwards that they would not go upstairs until his 'wife' came, and desired him to shew his friends the crown to pass the time till then. As soon as they were entering the room where the crown was kept, and the door was shut and locked behind them, as regulations required, they threw a cloak over the old man's head and clapped a gag into his mouth, which was a great plug of wood with a small hole in the middle to take breath at. This was tied on with a waxed leather which went round his neck. At the same time they fastened an iron hook to his nose that no sound might pass from him that way neither.

When they had thus secured him from crying, they told him their resolution was to have the crown, globe (Orb) and sceptre. And that, if he would quietly submit to it, they would spare his life; otherwise he was to expect no mercy. He therefore forced himself to make all the noise that possibly he could, to be heard above. Then they knocked him down with a wooden beetle (mallet) and told him that if yet he would lie quietly they would spare his life, but if not, on the next attempt to discover them, they would kill him, and they pointed three daggers at his breast. But he strained himself to make the greater noise; whereupon they gave him nine or ten more strokes upon the head with the mallet, for that many bruises were found upon his skull, and stabbed him into the belly.

Whereat the poor man, almost eighty years of age, fell and lay some time entranced. One of them kneeled on the ground to try if he breathed and not perceiving any breath come from him, said 'He is dead, I'll warrant him.' Mr Edwards came a little to himself, heard his words, and conceived it best for him to be so thought, and lay quietly. Then one of them named Parrot, a dyer out of Thames Street, put the globe into his breeches. Blood held the crown under his cloak. The third man was designed to file the sceptre in two, because it was too long to carry, and when filed it was to be put in a bag brought for that purpose.'

In modern terminology, it seems that an incident then occurred which was more worthy of a modern TV melodrama, for at that very moment, as the miscreants were hiding the precious items about their persons, who should arrive at the Martin Tower but Mr Edward's son! He had just returned from Flanders, where he had accompanied Sir Gilbert Talbot, and on landing in England had asked permission to visit his family. On approaching the Jewel House he saw the man who was guarding the downstairs entrance and naturally enquired what he wanted. The man replied that he belonged to the house, but young Edwards said that if he had any business with his father, he would go and tell him; and so he went up to the family apartment, to be welcomed by his mother, wife and sister.

Realising the game was up, the lookout rushed into the Jewel House (which consisted mainly of one large room) and on telling the others what had happened, they all rushed out of the building, taking the crown and orb with them but abandoning the sceptre as being too large to conceal. As they ran out, the old man regained consciousness and as his hands had not been tied, he pulled the gag out of his mouth and shouted 'Treason – Murder!'.

On hearing his cry, his daughter ran down and seeing her father had been wounded, ran out on the Parade (now the Broadwalk) and raised the alarm by shouting 'Treason, the crown is stolen!'. She was joined, not only by young Edwards and a Captain Beckman, old Mr Edwards' son-in-law, who had come for the betrothal celebration, but by just about everyone else in the vicinity. Soldiers dropped the weapons they were cleaning, warders deserted their posts, servants ran out of the Lieutenant's Lodgings, and it was even reported that in the confusion one soldier was about to shoot Captain Beckman as he ran past, until prevented from doing so by a warder! Beckman himself saved another warder, evidently not in uniform, from being injured by young Edwards who, mistaking him for one of the gang, was endeavouring to throttle him!

All joined in the chase after Blood and his companions, who were now heading towards the Byward Tower and ultimate freedom. A warder on duty at the drawbridge just beyond the Byward braced himself and prepared to detain the fleeing robbers, but Blood aimed his pistol and fired, and although the warder was unhurt, he wisely threw himself out of the way as they ran past him. At the far end of the drawbridge a sentinel named Sill, who had been a soldier under Cromwell, saw them coming but, having heard the shot and deciding that discretion was the better part of valour, made no effort to stop them.

The robbers had left their horses in the charge of Thomas Hunt, Blood's son-in-law, at the Iron Gate, renamed the East Gate, where Tower Bridge now stands, and so once clear of the Tower's outposts, the fugitives turned left and ran along Tower Wharf with Captain Beckman, young Edwards, together with warders and soldiers in hot pursuit. As usual the Wharf was crowded with passers-by, wharfingers, dockers and ferryboat men going about their various occupations and at the uproar they stood and stared with surprise at the 'parson' and his colleagues who, as if chasing some wrong-doers, ran past them, pointing ahead and shouting 'Stop the rogues!'

After they had covered some distance, Blood realised that the Captain was gaining on them so he half turned and discharged his second pistol at his pursuer, but Beckman swerved and, reaching out, managed to grab his assailant's cloak and, wrestling him to the ground, soon overpowered him. At that the older man admitted defeat, exclaiming ruefully 'It was a gallant attempt, however unsuccessful, for it was for a Crown'. Parrot, out of breath and slowing down, was quickly caught, as were the other gang members.

In the hectic struggle on the Wharf a large pearl, a diamond, and several smaller stones were dislodged from their settings in the crown, but the pearl was subsequently picked up by a sweeper and the diamond was handed in by an apprentice – honesty indeed! Some of the lesser gems were later recovered, and the balas-ruby, broken off the sceptre, was found in Parrot's pocket, so no stones of major importance were lost. It must be admitted by the author that, despite surreptitious searches among the cobbles whilst on duty patrolling the Wharf, none of the other lost gems were found, much to his disappointment!

At the sounds of the frenzied chase Thomas Hunt, waiting with the horses at the Iron Gate, promptly whipped up his horse and fled, it being reported that such was his breakneck speed and the need to look over his shoulder for possible pursuers, that he failed to notice a inn sign which, like those of so many establishments in the City, projected well out into the narrow lanes, and so was swept unceremoniously out of the saddle. As he lay half-stunned, a crowd gathered and, being recognised by a cobbler as a n'er-do-well, he was seized and marched to the house of a nearby Justice of the Peace.

While being questioned, news of the fracas at the Tower spread, and on hearing the news, a constable was detailed to march Hunt back to the scene of the crime and hand him over to the warders.

After the capture of Blood and the rest of the gang, young Edwards went straight to Sir Gilbert, who then rode to the palace at Whitehall to inform the King. Edwards, accompanied by officers of the Tower, proceeded to the White Tower where 'Blood lay in a corner, dogged and cowering and would not give a word of answer to any one question'. The King was persuaded to hear the examination at Whitehall and although no details of the proceedings are available, it is evident that the scoundrel succeeded in ingratiating himself with the monarch, apparently by saying he once plotted to assassinate the King but on seeing him, just couldn't bring himself to pull the trigger of the carbine! Another allegation suggested that Blood threatened the Monarch by implying that if he was executed, others would avenge his death. Whatever ensued at that hearing before Charles, his brother James and other members of the Court on 12 May, sufficient to say that he was released on 18 July and pardoned on 1 August.

Rumours to account for such unbelievable leniency quickly circulated. One was to the effect that the King, known to be short of money, had chosen this method of stealing his own Crown with the intention of detaching the stones and selling them on the Continent; another, that it was the outcome of a bet whereby the King had wagered no-one could steal it and the colonel had taken up the challenge. Some sources declared that Blood had been released because, politics being in turmoil, the King realised that it would be useful to have such an unscrupulous rogue on his payroll, while others swore that Blood, long suspected of being a government spy, may have known too much of the monarch's affairs, so making a public trial unthinkable. Whatever the reason, the fact remains that the lands of which Blood had been deprived in 1660 for being a Roundhead were restored to him, he was re-admitted to Court and was granted a pension of £500 a year! His fellow conspirators were also released without charge.

Not so lucky was Talbot Edwards for his spirited defence of the treasures, or those who had captured the villains. Edwards and his son were given grants of £200 and £100 respectively but finding difficulty in cashing them, had to sell them for half their value in order to pay for the medical treatment required by the injured Jewel House Keeper. Talbot died three years after the attack and was buried in the Chapel Royal of St Peter ad Vincula in the Tower, a stone bearing the inscription 'Here lieth the body of Talbot Edwards Gentn. late keeper of his mats. regalia who dyed ye 30 of September 1674 aged 80 yeares and 9 moneths' being set in the south wall of that Chapel.

Although later becoming a Quaker, Colonel Blood continued to sail close to the wind, libelling the Duke of Buckingham, his Lordship obtaining damages against him of £100,000, a verdict which resulted in Blood being thrown into prison for debt, though he was soon freed on bail. But the effect must have been too much for him, and after fourteen days illness he died on 29 August 1680 at his house at the corner of Peter Street and Tufton Street, Westminster. Two days later he was quietly buried in New Chapel Yard, Broadway, Westminster, but even though his demise was announced, his reputation was such that many suggested the corpse was not his and that he had some ulterior motive for dropping out of society. The contemporary historian Cunningham said 'dying and being buried were considered by the common people as a new trick on the part of their old friend the Colonel. So the coroner was sent for, the body taken up, and a jury summoned. There was some difficulty at first in identifying the body but finally the length of the left thumb which, in Blood's lifetime, was known to be twice its proper size, set the matter, like the corpse, everlastingly at rest; the jury separated, and the notorious Colonel was restored to his grave again'.

In 1865 the author John Timbs stated that the Literary Fund Society possessed, in their house on Adelphi Terrace, London, the two daggers carried by Blood and Parrot, describing them as beautifully chased and inlaid, with handles of a dark red wood and sheaths of embossed leather. Blood's dagger, the larger one of the two, was engraved with a griffin-like figure and dated 1602; Parrot's was engraved with the fleur-de-lys on each side.

Subsequently, as visitors are well aware, security of the Jewels have been markedly increased, and any would-be 'Colonel Bloods' are assured that, far from receiving a royal pension and being received at Court, a lengthy sojourn in other of Her Majesty's official hostelries would be made freely available! Why Colonel Blood did not find himself confined in one, is a mystery to this very day.

13. Where is the Body of Simon, Lord Lovat?

Simon Fraser, Lord Lovat was born in 1667 and as a youth he lived in Paris, where he became a Roman Catholic. There is little doubt that he was born a rebel, his later exploits making him one of the few people to have been imprisoned in both the Bastille and the Tower of London. As early as 1706, at the last session of the Scottish Parliament, Lord Belhaven described Captain Fraser, as he was then, as 'deserving, if practicable, to have been hanged five several times, in five different places and upon five different accounts at least, as having been a traitor to the Court of St James, a traitor to the Court of St Germains, a traitor to the Court of Versailles and a traitor to his own country of Scotland.'

And during the next forty years Lord Lovat changed little; although not taking an active role in the Jacobite Uprising of 1745, he had kept up a correspondence with the Young Pretender, and this eventually cost him his life. When he was captured on the Isle of Moran after the Battle of Culloden, he was so infirm that he had to be borne on a litter between the various towns *en route* to London. For the final journey to the Tower, however, he travelled in style, riding in an open landau drawn by six horses, accompanied by an officer and escorted by members of Liguier's cavalry regiment.

Where today the tablet commemorating the public execution site on Tower Hill stands, on 15 August 1746 the scaffold was ready and waiting for the imminent execution of his fellow lords, Balmerino and Kilmarnock, the structure surrounded by immense stands erected for the benefit of the thousands who would flock to see the savage decapitation of the Scottish captives, a sight to daunt even the doughty heart of Simon Fraser.

For four months he languished in the Tower awaiting trial until eventually, on 18 December, he was transported to the House of Lords by coach, guarded by an officer and thirty-six soldiers, with a yeoman warder at each door and General Williamson, Deputy Lieutenant of the Tower and the Yeoman Gaoler bearing the ceremonial axe sitting with him. Despite the escort 'the Hatred of the Mobb was So great to him' reported General Williamson 'that they broke both windows of My Coach in which he was, and I with him, and threw in Stones and dirt upon us, but did us no harm'. Despite his desperate predicament his ribald sense of humour never deserted him. When the coach slowed down a woman looked in through the shattered window and exclaimed 'You ugly old dog, don't you think you will have that frightful head cut off?' He replied 'You ugly old .... (bitch?), I believe I shall!' In court he declared that had he not been so old and infirm, they would have found it difficult to keep him there (in the Tower) and when told that they had confined much younger men there, he riposted 'Yes, but they were inexperienced; they had not broke so many gaols as I have!' At the conclusion of the trial he was found guilty by the unanimous verdict of 117 peers, and on 19 December he was sentenced to death.

Back at the Tower, while in conversation with General Williamson, he referred to his eldest son whom he had forced to join the rebellion, and commented jocularly 'We will hang him and then my second son shall marry your niece!' When the Major of the Tower asked him how he felt, he replied 'Why, I am about doing very well, for I am preparing myself, Sir, for a place where hardly any Majors and very few Lieutenant Generals go!'

He had earlier petitioned the King that if found guilty 'he may be executed after the manner of the Scots nobility i.e. by an Engine called the Maiden, which falls with great Velocity and at one blow severs the Head from the Body' but this plea was rejected and so Lovat had the doubtful claim to fame of being the last man to be executed by the axe in this country (the 'Scottish Maiden', the guillotine-like machine to which he referred, has survived and is displayed in the Edinburgh Museum – Author).

As was usual in those days, many months elapsed before the execution day finally arrived, and it was not until 1 April that the Royal Warrant affirmed that 'Lord Lovat stands attainted of high treason and for the same is to undergo and suffer the pains and forfeitures of high treason which by the laws and customs of this realm is to be drawn hanged and quartered and the said Simon Lord Lovat by law is to suffer death as aforesaid; yet his body now remaining in our Tower of London and at our will and pleasure and by the authority of our power royal, to be executed in such order and form as we think most convenient.' Writs were also issued for the handing over of the prisoner to the Sheriff of London and Middlesex at the Tower gates, and also to the Sheriffs, commanding them to cause the head of Lovat to be cut and stricken off and clearly severed from his body, on Tower Hill.

On Thursday 9 April 1747 the stands surrounding the scaffold started to fill up rapidly with avid spectators, so many in fact that one stand collapsed under the weight of the thousand people it bore, nearly a dozen of them (some reports said fifty) being killed outright and many others sustaining broken arms and legs. Among those killed were the carpenter who had erected the stand and his wife who had been selling liquor beneath it. Spectators clung like flies to surrounding roofs and balconies, even clinging precariously to the masts and rigging of ships moored at Tower Wharf.

Lovat had woken at three o'clock that morning and after a prayer, ordered that the Tower barber should comb out his wig genteely; while that was being done, he breakfasted on minced veal and drank his friends' health in wine and water. At length he was escorted by his two warders out of the Tower and up the hill through the jostling crowds. On being assisted up the scaffold steps he observed the vast multitude of spectators and exclaimed 'God help us! Why should there be such a bustle about taking off an old grey head that cannot get up three steps without two men to support it?'. Seeing the axe (the one currently on display in the Tower), he felt the edge of it and, instead of giving the executioner, John Thrift, his hat, gold-headed cane, his wig and clothes, to which the man was nominally entitled, he gave him ten gold guineas in lieu, having bequeathed his apparel to his cousin William Fraser. He then walked over to the coffin placed in readiness for his body, and read the inscription thereon 'Simon, Dominus Fraser de Lovat, decollat. April 9, 1747, aetat. suae 80'. Next, removing his hat and wig, he gave them to his cousin, reminding him again not to give them to the executioner.

Ordering his cap to be put on and loosening his neckcloth and shirt collar, he knelt down at the block, but Thrift considered he was too close to it and, with the warders' help – Lovat was, after all, eighty years of age – he moved further back. As was usual at such tragic moments, he then told the executioner he would say a short prayer and when ready, would let fall the handkerchief he was holding. When he did so, John Thrift brought down the heavy axe so accurately that he severed the head from the body at one blow. Rather than be allowed to fall on the sand-strewn boards of the scaffold, the head was caught in a white cloth held by two of those present, and contrary to the general custom, was not exhibited at the four corners of the scaffold to the crowds but was placed in the coffin together with the torso. Later, as witnessed by George Selwyn, a fashionable wit and politician whose hobby was regularly to attend executions, the head was to be sewn back on to the body and plans for the burial initiated. It was at this point that confusion started, confusion which developed into the mystery concerning the eventual whereabouts of Simon, Lord Lovat's corpse.

While in the Tower, he had expressed his desires regarding the disposal of his body in a letter sent to his cousin William (who was also his solicitor) requesting 'that you will order my Body to be carefully put up in a lead coffin after my execution and there to be preserved and ordered to be transported to the House of Muniack where the same is to lay for a night or two and then interr'd under my own Tomb in the Church of Kirkhill, and as soon as the corpse arrive at Inverness you are to order any two of my Friends you think proper, to invite so many of my friends and relations as you in consert with others shall advice to attend my Funerals.' Nor was he content with just a letter, for in a codicil in his will, he had ordered that all the pipers from John o' Groats to Edinburgh were to play before his corpse, for which they were to have a handsome allowance, and though he did not expect this wish to be complied with, yet he said he hoped that the good old women of his country would sing a 'coronach' before him.

As vast numbers of people were still milling around the scaffold site, William and another relative, James Fraser, deemed it safer to have the coffin taken back into the Tower for the time being, and when the crowds eventually dispersed, an undertaker named Stevenson, employed by the Frasers, requested that he might take the coffin to his funeral parlour in the City. Unaware of the order issued by the Secretary of State, the Duke of Newcastle, that the coffin should remain in the Tower, General Williamson, with the knowledge of the Constable of the Tower, Lord Cornwallis, granted the undertaker permission, that gentleman wasting no time in conveying it to his house in the Strand – where he proceeded to remove the lid and exhibit the body to eager members of the public for a substantial admission fee!

The execution of Lord Lovat on Tower Hill

Four days elapsed before news of this outrage eventually reached the General's ears and having reported it to the Constable, he notified the Duke of Newcastle on 13 April, referring to 'the great indignity as well as the indecencie of it – a thing never before heard of'.

It was at this point that William Fraser submitted a letter to the Duke quoting Simon Fraser's last wishes and endorsing it with his own request that he might therefore collect the coffin and take it North. He concluded by saying that as he had already arranged with Hugh Inglis, the owner of *The Pledger*, a ship then moored in the Thames, to transport the coffin to Inverness, he hoped for a speedy reply from the Government.

The Cabinet met on 15 April and their Lordships decided to reject William Fraser's request; the remains of Lord Lovat should be interred in the Tower. Accordingly, the following day the Duke of Newcastle wrote to the Tower authorities 'Mr. Stevenson, the undertaker in whose custody the body of Lord Lovat now remains, being directed to convey the same to the Tower of London and there to deliver it into your hands in order to its being interred, I am commanded to signify to you His Majesty's pleasure that you do accordingly receive the said body from Mr Stevenson and that you take care that it be interred within the Tower in a private manner.'

Pressure having been obviously brought to bear from some responsible quarter on the entreprenurial funeral director, the lid had been soldered down on the lead coffin and, a week after it had been removed from the Tower, it was duly returned, to be then interred in the Chapel Royal of St Peter ad Vincula within the Tower on 17 April, Good Friday, and the relevant entry was made in the register of burials.

There it remained until 1876 when, during restoration of the Chapel, it and many others, were removed from beneath the floor and relocated in the crypt. The lead coffin plate was detached from the lid and, together with those of the Earl of Kilmarnock and Lord Balmerino, is now displayed in a glass case affixed to the west wall, thereby allowing visitors to see the very plate that Lord Lovat himself read while on the scaffold. Beneath the case is an old paving stone clearly inscribed with two circles and a lozenge joined by a straight line. This stone once marked the precise position of the interment of Lord Lovat and his fellow lords and is presumed to have been marked in this way many decades ago by some member of the Tower garrison in sympathy with the Jacobite cause.

So the tragic drama would seem to have been terminated satisfactorily in accordance with regulations; the entry was made in the register entry and the coffin duly interred. But what, if anything, is actually in the coffin? In a letter to *Notes and Queries* of December 1884 a descendant, Sir William Fraser, claimed that Lovat's corpse was taken by night to Kirkhill near Inverness, and that only weeks before penning his letter he had actually seen the lead coffin in question. Moreover there was strong local tradition that the head, detached from the stitches which attached it to the torso, was contained in a small tin box deposited in the church vault, this fact being strongly supported by local people as recently as the early years of this century, although they stated that it had recently disappeared.

So does the coffin in the Tower's crypt contain the remains of Lord Lovat – or was the undertaker bribed to transfer the remains to another coffin for shipment to Scotland, then solder down the lid of an empty coffin? He had more than ample time, and when it was eventually returned for burial, the Tower authorities failed to open the coffin and check. One question leads to another – was the 'spare' coffin delivered to the Tower really empty, or had Stevenson filled it with stone as ballast – or perhaps even used it for a pauper's cadaver? If not, surely those who in 1876 moved it into the crypt must have detected the difference in weight from the others they handled, despite it being of lead. Or was Sir William Fraser duped by the coffin he reported seeing in 1884 – did it in fact have a body in it, and if so, whose was it? The answers will never be known.

14. Who Murdered King Henry VI in the Wakefield Tower?

In the evening of 21 May each year, since time immemorial, a special ceremony is re-enacted in the Oratory of the Wakefield Tower, known as the Ceremony of the Lilies and the Roses. Those present are the Resident Governor and the Chaplain of the Tower of London, the Provosts of Eton College and King's College, Cambridge or their representatives, clad in their magnificent robes, a small party of distinguished guests, and the Yeoman Warder appointed Clerk of the Chapels Royal or another member of the Chapel Council deputising for him, bearing the Chapel mace and clad in the scarlet and gold-embroidered coat of his State Dress uniform with the blue trousers of his undress uniform but wearing neither his sword nor Tudor bonnet. The Provosts each carry flowers. Because in the coat of arms belonging to Eton College appear three English lilies symbolic of Our Lady's innocence, so the Provost of that college carries Eton lilies bound up in light blue silk; in that of King's College, Cambridge, 'three roses argent' symbolises her Love; hence the Provost bears that number of those blooms bound with a purple ribbon. After the Divine Service, taken by the Chaplain, the flowers are placed in the little oratory of the chamber and left there for twenty-four hours, after which they are removed and burned.

Why such a ceremony? And why specifically there? Because it was in that very Tower, in 1471, that the body of Henry VI, the gentle and learned King who had founded Eton College in 1440 and King's College in 1441, was found brutally stabbed to death. During the service a prayer composed by the tragic King is read, and the 'certain place' where the blooms are laid is the spot where his lifeless body was discovered. But why would anyone want to murder such a man – or perhaps even more importantly, who DID murder him? The motives were complex, the reward was the throne of England – but the identity of the killer can only be guessed at.

Henry was crowned in Westminster Abbey in 1429 at the age of eight and again in Paris the following year, the Earl of Warwick being

Henry VI

his mentor and advisor. On achieving manhood he proved to be weak and vacillating, at times even mentally unstable, and so lacked the regal qualities essential in controlling the many factions vying for power at that time. Like many early monarchs he occasionally found himself short of funds, and in 1439 he pledged the Crown Jewels to his uncle Henry, Bishop of Winchester, as security for a loan of 7000 marks, agreeing that if he had not redeemed the loan by Easter of the following year, they would become the Bishop's property! Fortunately for the nation, the loan was repaid and the Jewels returned to the Jewel House!

Under Henry's feeble leadership, by 1453 the Hundred Years War with France ended with disastrous results for England, all our French possessions being lost with the exception of Calais. Worse was to follow for civil war broke in this country, the 'War of the Roses' between the rival houses of York and Lancaster. After a series of indecisive battles, Henry was captured at the battle of Northampton and forced to acknowledge Edward, Duke of York as heir to the throne. His Queen and supporters continued the bitter struggle until vanquished, victory finally going to the Yorkists in 1461 when Edward proclaimed himself king and was crowned Edward IV. Henry fled first to Scotland, then came south to take refuge on the borders of Lancashire and Yorkshire, evading arrest by adopting a disguise. But his foes eventually tracked him down and upon being captured in 1465 by one Thomas Talbot, the King, triumphant and vindictive, consigned him to the Tower in disgrace. The captive's gilt spurs were struck off and, wearing a placard on his back and a straw hat on his head, his legs tied to the stirrups of his horse, his mount was then paraded three times round a tree in front of the Tower to shame him still further while the crowds jeered in derision.

He was confined in the Wakefield Tower, which was categorised at that time as being 'a prison for harmless men', where he was treated humanely and with respect. Bills in existence testify to his welfare, one Robert Radcliffe being paid 40s 'for expenses of Henry of Windsor, late in deed but not of right, king of England'. Further comforts were permitted, Henry being allowed to have his pet sparrow and favourite dog for company. And there, resigned to his fate, he remained for long five years.

In 1470, fate favoured him once more, and he was restored to power by the influence of the Earl of Warwick but alas, his new-found freedom was short-lived. Only a year later Warwick suffered defeat at the Battle of Barnett and Henry was once more sent to the Tower. Re-entering his old quarters in the Wakefield Tower on Easter Sunday 1471, he found the authorities as considerate as before, the accounts showing that the cost of his keep and that of ten attendants amounted to £14.5s plus an additional 3s 6d a day for the 'hire and board of three readers who came to beguile him'. But their services were soon to become unnecessary, for on 22 May, the day after Edward IV returned to London from the country, Henry was found lying in the oratory, having apparently been stabbed to death while at prayer.

The body was left for one night in the Chapel Royal of St John in the White Tower, then taken out and exposed at the Cross in Cheapside so that everyone would know the King was dead. According to Dr Warkworth, when the corpse was subsequently taken to St Paul's Cathedral it bled profusely with his face open i.e. uncovered, and this happened again when it was carried into Blackfriars' Monastery. From there it was later taken at midnight by barge on the River Thames to Chertsey Abbey, the craft being accompanied by others, some occupants carrying blazing torches, others being monks chanting dirges. The body was buried in the Abbey 'without priest or clerke, torch or taper, singing or saying'. The remains were later ordered to be re-interred in St George's Chapel, Windsor Castle on the orders of Richard when he became King in 1483. Near the vault a flagstone bears the words 'King Henry VI' and a stone bearing the King's name and the date of his death is inlaid in the floor of the oratory in the Wakefield Tower, on which the lilies and the roses are placed during the Ceremony mentioned earlier. Two decades later, King Henry VII proposed that the dead martyr be canonised but this lapsed shortly afterwards; the appeal however is believed to have been renewed by the members of the Henry VI Society.

The identity of the assassin was never discovered, some authorities even disputing the cause of death. The historian Hume suggested that the King 'expired in confinement but whether he died a natural death or a violent one is uncertain'. The Monk of Croyland in his *Chronicles* was non-commital, at first restricting himself to saying simply 'the body of the King was found lifeless in the Tower', although later he declared that Henry 'was strykked with a dagger in the hands of the Duke of Gloucester'. Yet another historian, Fleetwood, averred that the King died 'of pure displeasure and melancholy on May 25'.

Other authorities were in no doubt, most accusing Richard, Duke of Gloucester as being personally responsible. The historian Polydore Virgil declared that Richard slew him with a sword – although up to the time of the Reformation the Warden of Caversham used to show visitors 'the holy(!) dagger that killed King Henry'! The precise time of death was defined in Dr Warksworth's chronicle, which stated that 'Henry VI was put to death on 21 May, on a Tuesday night between eleven and twelve of the clock', he also pointing an accusing finger at Richard. This was echoed by rumours to the effect that the King died, 'the Duke of Gloucester then being at the Tower and many others'. Could the fact that Richard had Henry's remains transferred to the Royal Chapel at Windsor Castle in 1483 be taken as a sign of remorse by the man alleged to be the murderer? Some factions declared that Richard only acted as a 'contract killer', S R Gardiner writing 'There can be no reasonable doubt that he was murdered, and that, too, by Edward's directions'.

On the other hand there were some who proclaimed Richard's innocence, declaring that Henry had been found dead, not on 21 May but on 24th or even 26th of that month, dates when Richard was not in London but at Sandwich in Kent. They support their argument by pointing to the Tower's records which showed that food and necessities were provided for him 'for fifteen days beginning 11 May', these proving that he must therefore have been alive until 26th May (unless the accounts had been falsified for the financial

The Wakefield Tower

benefit of the caterers and others involved!).

So did the first King of England to die in the Tower of London succumb to a natural or violent death? Exactly when? And by whose hand? Yet another of the many imponderable enigmas which baffle the seekers after truth.

15. Four Knights who met Sudden Death

Anne Boleyn and Katherine Howard were accused by Henry VIII of having affairs with other men, but the King himself was no paragon of virtue, for rumour had it that he dallied with, as they say, a lady at Court by the name of Mary Berkley. Rumour went even further, alleging that in about 1527, the year in which he started negotiating with the Pope for a divorce from Katherine of Aragon, Mary bore him a son, John. In due course the lady married a Thomas Perrot, John taking his surname and later was knighted, such royal patronage giving further credence to his claims of regal descent. Indeed judging by contemporary reports Sir John strongly resembled the King in looks and in nature, being described as being 'of stature and size far beyond the ordinary man; he seems never to have known what fear was, and distinguished himself by martial exercises'. It was related that during a boar hunt in France in 1551, he rescued one of the hunters from the attack of a wild boar 'giving the boar such a blow that it did well-nigh part the head from the shoulders'. In his attitude too, observers detected the similarity, for he was arrogant and headstrong, nor did he suffer fools gladly. He was not lacking in courage, and became a valiant soldier, being appointed Lord-Deputy in Ireland in 1584, where he did much to restore order and a certain amount of prosperity in that troubled country.

Despite the sterling qualities he possessed, nevertheless he made enemies, chief among them being Adam Loftus, Archbishop of Armagh and Dublin and the Lord Chancellor Sir Christopher Hatton (after whom Hatton Garden was named). Sir John always claimed kinship with Henry, this claim also being accepted later by Queen Elizabeth I who looked on him as her 'half-brother', giving him gifts of jewels and even going so far as to wave to him familiarly from her window in Greenwich Palace as he sailed along the Thames in his elaborate barge. But Elizabeth was subject to mercurial mood swings, her subjects never knowing quite which way she would react in a given situation, and on one occasion Sir John failed to take this into consideration. Having chided him for a slight misdemeanour, she later became apprehensive about a possible Spanish army landing in Ireland preparatory to invading England and, changing her tune, complimented him on his achievements. Upon her volte-face, Sir John rashly exclaimed 'Ah, now she is ready to piss herself for fear of the Spaniard, I am once again one of her white boys!' Had this most improper remark been made in private among his intimate friends, all would have been well, but it was spoken in public, in Dublin! Such comments were grist to his enemies' mill. Not only did they ensure that the remark reach the ears of the Queen, but a false accusation of treason was levelled against him, resulting in his recall from Ireland in 1588 and inevitably, confinement in the Tower. At his trial in 1591 the only real evidence was that one unfortunate remark, but despite that he was found guilty of high treason. On being taken back to his prison with an escort of yeoman warders, he exclaimed angrily to Sir Owen Hopton, the Lieutenant of the Tower 'What! Will the Queen suffer her brother to be offered up as a sacrifice to the envy of my strutting adversary (Hatton)?' Elizabeth was equally outraged. Giving vent to one of her explosive Tudor rages, she vehemently declared 'that the jury which had brought in that verdict were all knaves, and that she would not sign the warrant for execution'.

Nor was he executed, but died under mysterious circumstances in the September of that year, the cause of death being conveniently attributed to 'a broken heart'. A friend, describing his final hours, said 'His haughtiness of spirit accompanied him to the last, and still, without any diminution of courage therein, it burst the bonds of his magnanimitie'. He was buried in the Chapel Royal of St Peter ad Vincula on 10 October 1591.

His death, whether by natural or violent means, must have pleased those who had directly or indirectly initiated not only his arrest and trial but perhaps even had connived at the guilty verdict. What could their motive have been? Did they fear that, should Elizabeth die, John would claim the throne and revenge himself upon them? In the maelstrom of Tudor intrigues, all things were possible.

Nor were Sir John's enemies content merely with ensuring his removal from the political scene; it will come as no surprise to learn that one of Sir John's officers, Sir Thomas Williams, was committed to the Tower with him – and also died, cause unknown, in August 1591, being buried in the Chapel on the 20th of that month. Yet another of his officers, Sir Thomas Fitzherbert, was committed to the

Tower on 10 January 1591, a warrant to the Lieutenant of the Tower stating 'These shall be to require you to receive into your safe custody the person of Sir Thomas Fitzherbert, knight, to be kept close prisoner in such strict sort as no manner of person be suffered to have access unto him without special direction from us; and touching the charges of the diet and otherwise of Sir Thomas Fitzherbert during his being with you, you shall take order with the said knight for the defraying thereof himself. And so requiring you to have due care in the performance hereof, we bid you farewell'. In other words, don't let anyone speak to him, and make sure he pays for his own food and other necessities.

Due to the close confinement his health deteriorated and upon being notified in June 1591, the Council granted him the Liberty of the Tower, ordering the Lieutenant to permit his prisoner 'to walk at some convenient time and place within the Tower in his company, or in the company of some trusted person whom he should appoint, so that no manner of person had access to him or conferred with him by any means'. But three months later, on 7 October that year, three days before the funeral of Sir John Perrot, he too died, from unspecified causes.

As if that were not enough to arouse the gravest suspicions, Sir Nicholas White, another close colleague of Sir John, was committed to the Tower on 9 March 1591, and was also granted the Liberty of the Tower, reportedly because of ill-health. He apparently survived for a further two years imprisonment before dying. Neither the cause of his death nor even its date, is recorded, the only evidence being a letter giving his son, Mr Nicholas White 'permission to convey the body of his father, lately deceased in prison, back to Ireland for burial'. Surely they couldn't ALL have died of broken hearts!

Musingly, one wonders whether Henry VIII ever contemplated marrying Mary Berkley, rather than Anne Boleyn, following the end of his marriage to Katherine of Aragon? Or whether, on learning that Edward, the son he desperately wanted to succeed him, born to his third wife Jane Seymour in 1537, was weak and sickly, he regretted not having done so, for union with Mary Berkley would have made John, a strapping and mature twenty year old youth at the time of Henry's death in 1547, his automatic successor, as King John II.

Had that come about, the course of history would have been radically altered. Anne Boleyn and Katherine Howard would not

Sir Thomas Fitzherbert

have become queens and so would not have been beheaded, neither would George Boleyn nor his widow Lady Rochford, Katherine Howard's lady-in-waiting.

Because Henry would not have married Jane Seymour either, there would have been no son Edward, hence Lady Jane Grey, her husband Lord Guildford Dudley and so many of her supporters would have escaped the scaffold.

'Bloody' Mary, child of Henry and Katherine of Aragon, would have been the equivalent of a princess royal and as such would have played second fiddle to King John II; therefore those who suffered so tragically for their religion during her reign would not have done so; nor would those victims of Elizabeth, daughter of Anne Boleyn, have perished, for she would not have been born! And as a consequence of that, Mary, Queen of Scots would never been decapitated in Fotheringhay Castle, Northants.

But was Sir John Perrot the son of Henry VIII? Did he really die of a broken heart? Who caused the deaths of his colleagues Sir Thomas Williams, Sir Thomas Fitzherbert and Sir Nicholas White in the Tower of London within a space of a few short months? And how did they die? Alas, the cold stones of the Tower never divulge their grim secrets.

16. Who Shot the Earl in the Bloody Tower?

To be imprisoned in the Tower once, is unfortunate, twice is asking for trouble and the third time, trouble is what one receives! Such was the experience of Sir Henry Percy who conspired with others supporting Mary, Queen of Scots and on 15 November 1571 was caught and sent to the Tower. During the following year it is likely that his yeoman warder asked him the Tudor equivalent of whether he'd like the bad news or the good news first, for his brother Sir Thomas Percy, 7th Earl of Northumberland, had also been plotting to place Mary Stuart on the English throne and although taking refuge in Scotland, had been captured in 1572 and beheaded. The good news was that Sir Henry was now the 8th Earl of Northumberland, although it is doubtful whether he would have celebrated the occasion, for a further year's imprisonment loomed ahead before he was released in May 1573 upon payment of a fine of 5000 marks (one mark being equivalent to about 66p in modern currency). It was a conditional discharge from custody for he was ordered not to leave his estate at Petworth, but that notwithstanding, he obviously had not learned his lesson; by 1582 he was once more involved in another plot, again in support of Mary Stuart, this time a conspiracy conceived by a zealous Catholic, Francis Throckmorton.

This plan in its turn was thwarted, for so efficient were Queen Elizabeth's intelligence gatherers that all the conspirators were rounded up and once again the great oak doors of the Tower closed behind the Earl. But at least he fared better than did Throckmorton. Following the discovery of incriminating documents in his house, Francis was escorted to the White Tower and severely racked but would admit nothing. Threatened again with the rack, he 'voluntarily' made a confession which he later withdrew, but it was too late; his confession was his death warrant, for he had divulged enough for the authorities to charge him with 'bringing in of Foreigners into England and deposing against the Queen'.

The dread consequences were inevitable. In the words of the historian Stow 'The 21. of May 1584, Francis Throckmorton Esquire was arraygned in the Guild hall of the cittie of London, where being found guiltie of high Treason, hee was condemned, & had judgement to be drawne, hanged, bowelled & quartered. The 10. of July next following, the same Francis Throckmorton was conveyed from the Tower of London, to the Black Fryers stayres, and from thence by land to the sessions hall in the Olde baily without (outside) Newgate, where hee was deliuered to the sheriffes of London, laid on a hurdle, drawn to Tyburn, & there executed according to his judgement'.

Meanwhile, back at the Tower Henry Percy   endured imprisonment for only a short while and then, probably because of lack of evidence, was given a second chance and released. But our determined nobleman just could not give up plotting and by 1583 he was involved with the 3rd Baron Paget in yet another intrigue supporting Mary. By now he must have been under permanent surveillance by the Queen's ever-watchful cohorts and, perhaps realising they were closing in on the group, the Earl helped the Baron and his family to escape to the Continent. But the game was up, for a go-between in those negotiations was one William Shelley who, arrested and brought to the White Tower, was 'persuaded' to reveal all. And as the 'all' directly involved Henry Percy, that nobleman was taken into custody on 15 December 1583 and three weeks or so later, on 9 January 1584, found himself under escort taking the by-now familiar journey to the prison he knew so well, there to be conducted to quarters in the Bloody Tower.

As befits an aristocrat, he was allowed his servants, three in number, consisting of Messrs. Palmer, Pantin and Price, to look after him over the next few months pending his appearing in the House of Lords where, if found guilty by his peers of high treason, he would not be placed on trial but would be attainted, a Bill of Attainder being passed which would deprive him of his civil rights, property and estates.

On 21 June his three menservants were removed and placed under arrest on some trumped up charge by Sir Christopher Hatton, their place being taken by one Thomas Bailitf. And it was he who, around midnight, raised the alarm, declaring that the Earl had committed suicide. Together with yeoman warders and soldiers, the Lieutenant of the Tower, Sir Owen Hopton rushed to the Bloody Tower and entered the bedroom, where he found the prisoner lying in his bed, the blankets drawn up in orderly fashion about his body. Pulling the bed-clothes down, Sir Owen was shocked to find

everything soaked in the blood which was oozing from three wounds in the Earl's torso.

Realising nothing could be done to save the man's life, he left the building to report the tragedy to his superiors. On doing so he noticed a pistol lying on the ground outside and Bailiff, standing nearby, immediately suggested that the Earl had shot himself, then thrown the weapon through the window. That this could have happened was instantly rejected out of hand by the Lieutenant, for how could a man so mortally wounded, hurl the weapon away, then arrange the bed-clothes neatly around himself? Moreover if he had committed suicide, why bother to do that?

At the inquest held by the Coroner of the Tower Ward, the Lieutenant's patently obvious suspicions were ignored, for it was declared 'that, on 16 June, the Earl had acquired through the services of James a Price, Yeoman, a dagge (a small pistol) of iron and steel of the value of twenty shillings, certain bullets of lead, and a quantity of gunpowder in a small box. These had been hidden in a mattress under the bolster until the aforesaid date'. Moreover this statement was confirmed by the gunsmith who had sold the items.

It was then stated that the Earl had bolted himself in his room 'lest any man should foresee or withstand his devilish, felonious and malicious intent and, not having theAlmighty God or his fear before his eyes, did take up into his hands the aforesaid Dagge of iron and steel, then and there made ready charged with gunpowder and three bullets of lead and place the aforesaid Dagge to the left part of his breast, near unto the pap of the same part of his breast .... and did discharge, by reason of the violence of which gunpowder and three bullets of lead, the aforesaid Earl into his body and heart and through his chin bone, even into his right shoulder, himself with the aforesaid bullets, did strike, giving unto himself one mortal wound of the depth of twelve inches and of the breadth of two inches, of which mortal wound the aforesaid Earl instantly died.'

The jury was then 'invited' to deliver the required verdict of suicide, the motive being recorded as the Earl's fear of being beheaded and the fact that by being attainted, his family would be deprived of their birthright, this latter allegedly confirmed by an earlier comment he had made in which he exclaimed 'The Bitch (Queen Elizabeth) shall not have my estates!'

But was it really suicide, or a murder arranged by those who, having had Throckmorton hanged, drawn and quartered, and Baron Paget forced to flee the country, wanted to remove the last of the troublesome and potentially dangerous trio, one who after all was in the Tower for the third time for the same offences against the Queen? Was there some reason to deny him challenging the treason charges in the House of Lords? Were there others plotting royal mischief, earls, perhaps even dukes, determined at all costs to remain undiscovered?

What of the evidence itself? Lacking today's forensic expertise, nevertheless much credence must be placed on the Lieutenant's conclusions that, having shot himself three times the Earl could not have possibly thrown the pistol through the window ('the aforesaid Earl instantly died' the Coroner's report had said).

That it was murder is self-evident by considering the 'beaten zone', the spread of the bullets. The Coroner's Court statement specifically declared that one shot hit the prisoner in the heart, another through the chin bone and a third in the right shoulder. Even had the Earl held the pistol at arm's length and pressed the trigger with his thumb, the spread of the wounds would have been negligible, the bullets entering almost through the same wound. But the wounds sustained by the prisoner were spread over such a comparatively wide area that the pistol must have been fired from further away, well beyond the reach of the victim's outstretched arm and hand.

The main suspect was of course Thomas Bailiff, who could easily have arranged the purchase of the weapon and not only the fabrication of the story regarding its concealment but also could have locked the bedroom door after the murder – if it was indeed locked; he must already have had a key, for he reported what he had actually seen to the Lieutenant. Did Bailiff carry out the murder himself, or did he admit an assassin to the bed chamber and help him to escape undetected in the ensuing confusion?

In order to carry out the operation successfully, the murderer, whoever he was, went to totally unnecessary lengths to ensure the Earl's death. A single shot through the sleeping victim's heart, the pistol then left by the body or clutched in his dead hand, the bedclothes in disarray, would have left no room for doubt that it was suicide. Why then, stand feet away and fire three bullets from a distance? If he had wanted to use that number of bullets to guarantee fatal results, then why not hold the barrel just inches away from the victim's heart?

A further factor in the argument against suicide is that the bodies of those who had taken their own life were by ancient custom buried in the City Ditch or at cross-roads, and certainly not in consecrated ground, yet Stow in his *Annals* states that after Henry Percy's death 'it remained to provide for his wretched carcase which, on the 23rd day of June 1585 was buried in St Peter's Church within the said Tower of London'. The defence rests its case.

17. The American Prisoner who claimed He was Poisoned

Edward Gove was American by domicile but English by birth, having been born in East Smithfield, London, in 1630. His father, John, a dealer in brass, and Mary, his mother, emigrated in 1647, taking Edward, his brother and his sister to America, the family first settling in Charlestown, in the Colony of Massachusetts Bay, and later moving to New Hampshire. John died in the following year, his will including such items as 'a great kettle weighing $21^1/_2$ lbs, little skellets & kettles with 2 skimers, $2^1/_2$ lbs of wyre and $34^1/_2$ lbs of oulde brasse', the proceeds from the sale of the latter commodity to be divided between Edward and his brother John. Following her husband's death, Mrs Gove married again but after her second husband died in 1671 she moved to Hampton, where Edward was then living, and spent the rest of her days there. But how on earth did this 'new' American find himself in the Tower? And who would want to poison him? For that we have to turn back the clock to see how such momentous and extraordinary events came about.

By 1660 Edward had become a prosperous landowner and in that year he married a local girl named Hannah. He had matured into an outspoken and blunt man; when he felt he was being wronged he wasted little time in taking action to put it right, using forceful language, even violent methods when he considered it necessary. In 1673 he was even arrested and fined for abusing a neighbour and calling him a thief. Because he was so forthright in his manner, and a local landowner as well, he became a freeman and represented New Hampshire in the assembly, eventually leading the party that was in opposition at that time.

Much of the territory in that area had been granted by a Royal Charter of 1622 to a London merchant, Captain John Mason, authorising him to 'plant, rule, order and govern New-England in America', but in 1635 he died, his grandson Robert Tufton Mason succeeding to the inheritance. Trouble had been brewing for some years because fishermen and other colonists, having bought much of the land from Indian chiefs, settled there, claiming it as their own by right or useage, it being in many cases, territory they had defended against a savage foe, and legal wrangling continued on and off until in 1679, New Hampshire was made a royal province, the president and members being appointed by the King, Charles II, its laws being made by the assembly, of which Edward Gove was a member. The immediate effect of this enactment was that Robert Mason claimed ownership of the estates to which he believed he had legal right. This demand was so strongly resisted by the settlers that Mason tried bullying and intimidation, assuming the title of Lord Proprietor and even forbidding them to cut timber to use as fuel. There was only one man strong enough in character to lead the dissidents in their fight for what they considered justice and so, on 21 March 1681, they made their obvious choice – Edward Gove!

Mason, infuriated by the resistance he had encountered and the refusal of the settlers, not only to surrender the property he considered to be his, but also their scornful rejection of his 'generous' offer to lease some of it to them, left the province and returned to England, determined by whatever means in his power to get his own way. What he sought was a man who, given a hundred and fifty pounds a year, with the mortgage of Mason's lands as security, plus the consideration to the King of twenty per cent of the rents collected, and granted the rank and title of lieutenant-governor and commander-in-chief of New Hampshire Province into the bargain, was capable of setting up the sort of administration he needed, a man whom he could manipulate to enforce his rights by force if necessary. Arriving back in London, he contacted his powerful friends at Court, through whom he had influence with the King himself; a word here, a hint there, and within a matter of months the very man emerged. His name was Edward Cranfield.

An ideal operator, one who would achieve results by fair means or foul, Cranfield was unprincipled, ruthless and, given the opportunity, utterly dictatorial in his methods. Arriving in the colony in 1682 he wielded the widespread powers given to him with an iron hand. One of his first decrees was to declare that all the settlers were to take up leases from Mason within one month, and such was their protests that Edward Gove decided to act on their behalf, declaring 'that his sword was drawn, and that he would not lay it down till he knew who should hold the government.'

At this mutinous show of defiance, Cranfield had to assert his authority and forthwith issued arrest warrants to his police officials, taking further precautions by placing the whole militia of the Province on standby. Easily eluding the constables sent to bring him in, Edward Gove, with his customary bravura, decided on confrontational tactics, and on 27 January 1683, with sword drawn, he led twelve mounted men into Hampton 'all armed with swords and pistols, with a trumpet sounding'. But he was not greeted by the overwhelming support he expected and so, doubtless bitterly disappointed, he and his men surrendered to the town authorities.

Cranfield was of course delighted. Placing them in irons (shackled around their ankles) and guarded by a strong party of mounted men, he then wrote to the Lords of Trade and Plantations in England that Edward Gove, having made it his business to stir up rebellion in the territory, had been arrested and he and his men would be tried by the laws of England on 1 February 1683.

At the preliminary examination Gove admitted that he did sound the trumpet or caused it to be sounded, as it was his own; likewise he drew his sword because it was his weapon, and went on to state that the governor was not a judge, but a pretender and traitor to the King and his authority. After that outburst, all were remanded in prison, from where Gove wrote to the justices, pleading false imprisonment and protesting against being shackled, the chains between the shackles being five feet long and locking two men together.

Meanwhile Governor Cranfield arraigned a court to be held in Portsmouth, in the Colony of New Hampshire, to try the accused, the charge, stripped of the legal verbiage, being that 'by the instigation of the Devil, they, having withdrawn their allegiance and obedience to our Sovereign Lord the King, did appear at Hampton in a rebellious body in a hostile manner and with treasonable words did incite the people to sedition and rebellion'. The prosecution further blackened Gove's character by testifying that 'some years since in a Strange Distemper Seemingly Lunatick, he did attempt to kill the wife of George Martin, Saying that shee bewitched him, and did to that end charged his pistolls'. For that offence he had been placed in safe custody to prevent him from doing hurt to himself or others, but those in charge of him said that the Distemper was still there and indeed his mother had died of it!

Edward Gove's companions of that ill-fated sortie explained how their leader had called them out, saying 'we have swords by our sides as well as others, and would see things mended before we will lay them down'. By now Gove must have realised that he was facing a charge of high treason with all its terrible implications and this was brought home to him in no uncertain fashion when, after all the evidence had been given, the jury retired to consider their verdict. After six hours, they returned, the foreman announcing their decision; all the defendants had been found guilty as charged.

Judge Richard Waldron proceeded to respite all the defendants except Gove, until the King should declare their punishment. Then, shedding tears as he did so, he passed sentence on the ringleader, saying;

'You, Edward Gove, shall be drawn on a hedge to the place of execution and there you shall be hanged by ye neck, and when yet living be cut down and cast on the ground, and your bowels shall be taken out of your belly, and your privy members be cut off and burnt while you are yet alive, your head shall be cut off and your body divided into four parts, and your head and quarters shall be placed where our Sovereign Lord the King pleaseth to appoint. And the Lord have mercy on your soul'.

To hear such a death sentence, one more suited to be pronounced in the High Court in the Old Bailey rather than in a far-distant colony on the American continent, must have been a blood-chilling experience, but worse was to follow, if that were possible, for Edward Gove's estate was also to be seized and forfeited to the Crown, his large family thereby being rendered destitute and penniless. As for his fellow mutineers, they later received pardons, for they 'were all young men and not realizing their transgressions, being altogether unacquainted with the laws of England'.

Governor Cranfield was now faced with an almost impossible dilemma. Even were he to find someone capable and willing to perform such an abhorrent execution, could he rely on the militia, themselves local men, to control a possible uprising by the colonists, riots which might even threaten his own authority, even his personal safety? There was only one thing to do – send the traitor to England; let 'them' execute him! Accordingly he directed Thomas Joules, commander of the ship *Richard of Boston* to convey Edward Gove to England, promising that twenty pounds would be paid to him upon the prisoner being safely handed over to the authorities on arrival. The Governor also sent a transcript of the trial to the officials in

Whitehall together with a letter explaining that 'I cannot with safety to my selfe or to the peace of the Province keepe him longer in custody for I have cause to feare the Souldiers in time may be remiss or overpowered and so Gove sett at liberty'. And no doubt breathing a sigh of relief at having got the leader of the troublemakers out of the way, he promptly reasserted his authority and increased the harshness of his regime by raising the local taxes and imprisoning without charge any who failed to comply.

The ship carrying Edward Gove arrived in England on 6 June 1683 and he was taken to the Tower of London. His wife had already sent a letter to King Charles begging that mercy be shown to her husband and Edward himself submitted a plea for clemency, apologising for his actions and requesting that some money from his sequestered estate be paid to him – one had little comfort or food in the Tower without adequate funds. Whether money was forthcoming is not known, but bills of expense for the safe keeping in the Tower of Edward Gove, together with those of a Lord Lorn, submitted by Thomas Cheek, Lieutenant of the Tower, are on file, one covering a period of sixteen weeks and seven days (sic), for the sum of £18 9s 5d, and another for the period 26 December 1685 to 10 March 1686 amounting to £7 2s 9 ^{3}/4d.

Despite the negotiations which were being carried on, all petitions for his pardon were refused, as he was under condemnation for high treason. Moreover his freedom of movement continued to be severely restricted and his ankles sorely chafed until 28 May 1684, when the King ordered that he be given greater freedom and allowed to walk within the walls, under escort. Accordingly, after having been shackled for more than a year, his irons were finally struck off by the Tower blacksmith. While the months dragged on, the question of an appeal was considered and eventually put before the Court at Whitehall, but it was not until 9 April 1685 that the prisoner under sentence of death was informed of a royal proclamation which stated;

'To the Lieutenant of the Tower; whereas Edward Gove was near three years since apprehended, tried and convicted in our Colony of New England in America and in June 1683 was Committed a prisoner in the Tower of London, We have thought fit hereby to Signify our will and pleasure to you that you cause him, the said Edward Gove to be inserted in the next general Pardon that shall come out for the poor convicts of Newgate, without any Condition of

Transportation (i.e. not to be sent to any of the penal colonies), he giving security for his good behaviour as you will think requisite and for so doing, this shall be your warrant. Given at our Court at Windsor the 14 day of September in the first year of our Reign. James R.'

Whether this pardon was the act of clemency by the newly crowned King, James II having succeeded to the throne, or whether it would have happened anyway, is immaterial; the fact remained that the imminent threat of an horrific execution no longer hung over Edward Gove's head, although he would have to remain in the Tower until the following Michaelmas when the general release of convicts took place.

Meanwhile, back in the American colony, conditions were going from bad to worse. Cranfield's tyrannical regime, designed to browbeat the settlers into submission, had the opposite effect. Demonstrations, even acts of violence, were the order of the day, it being reported that tax collectors were greeted with scalding water from the women and with clubs by the men, and in one instance an official, endeavouring to collect his dues on a Sunday, was promptly felled by a young girl wielding her Bible!

But a happy ending for all was in sight – except for Governor Cranfield. Nathaniel Weare, the people's agent, travelled to London and there presented the King with detailed and scathing reports of Cranfield's arbitrary dealings and autocratic methods. Substantiated by other leading citizens, the report so convinced the King, that His Majesty not only censured Cranfield, but removed him from office, and when the unexpected news reached the Colony, a self-constituted committee went to his quarters and escorted him out of town with a rope around his neck, his legs tied under his horse's belly, and minus his sword! The King also sent a letter from Whitehall dated 12 April 1686 to the President and Council of the Colony stating that he had granted a full pardon to Edward Gove and requiring them to restore to him all his forfeited estates.

Now free from Cranfield's jurisdiction, the Council willingly complied with this royal instruction and went even further. At a meeting of the Council in Boston on 9 November 1686 it was agreed that 'a Report be made unto His Majesty of Edw. Cranfield's Estate in New England, and what money was received by him of such persons as purchased the estate of Edward Gove'.

So the baddy got his come-uppance and Edward, the local hero, returned in triumph to his family and grateful friends, there to resume a now-enhanced place in New Hampshire society. It was recorded that on the ship bringing him back in 1686 he brought a pear tree which he planted on his Hampton estate and which was reportedly still bearing fruit as recently as the 1920s.

A story with a happy ending indeed – or was it? Edward Gove died in Hampton on 29 July 1692 aged sixty-two years of age, maintaining to the end that slow poison had been administered to him during the long fraught years he had been incarcerated in the Tower of London. The State Prison's cuisine was never noted for its gourmet quality, to say the least, but could his allegation have been true? Who would have attempted it – Robert Mason, in order to take no chances of a reprieve but to remove once and for all the man who posed the greatest threat to his ambitions? He certainly had the influence and wealth to bribe those who had food-shops on Tower Hill, even avaricious employees within the Tower itself, to doctor the prisoner's food. Governor Cranfield too must have feared Gove's possible return and the consequential violent backlash from his sworn enemy's supporters. He too had his contacts in London; did he, perhaps even in collaboration with Mason, seek to destroy the one man who could, and indeed did, bring about his downfall? And will we ever know?

To end with another debatable point – is Edward Gove eligible for inclusion in the Guiness Book of Records as the first – and only – 'American' ever to have been sentenced to be hanged, drawn and quartered?

18. Suicide on Tower Green –
Or was it Murder?

In the 1680s political turmoil raged in England. Charles II professed to be a member of the Church of England, although on his death-bed he proved to be a Roman Catholic. His younger brother James, Duke of York, was an avowed Papist, and so many of the upper classes believed fervently that the country was secretly becoming a dependency of the French King and under the religious auspices of the Pope. In order to rectify this situation, one faction was in favour of violent action, in other words the assassination of the Royal pair, thereby clearing the way for James, Duke of Monmouth, to be King. Others advocated more peaceful methods such as exile for the brothers.

Matters came to a head however, in 1683, with the Rye House Plot. The hot-headed faction conspired to ambush the King and James, Duke of York, as they returned from Newmarket races, the plan being facilitated by the fact that one of the plotters owned Rye House Farm, near Hoddesdon in Hertfordshire, this being on the royal route. The attack itself would be easy; one member of the group would block the narrow road with a cart, others would open fire from behind a nearby wall, spreading confusion among the royal party, and then attackers on horseback would charge and kill any survivors. Their strategy was well conceived – their security was not, for advance warning had reached the authorities and the plan failed completely.

Needless to say, the Government's reaction was swift and merciless, not only the advocates of violence being rounded up but also the others who preferred to change the royal line by political manipulation and peaceful persuasion. Many of those not implicated in the Plot were arrested and accused of high treason, among them being Lord Russell, Algernon Sidney, and the Earl of Essex. The latter, Arthur Capel, was no skulking conspirator lurking in the shadows; on the contrary he was one of the most popular liberal leaders in the country and had been Ambassador to Copenhagen, Lord Lieutenant of Ireland and even, for a short time, Prime Minister. But that mattered little when the fear of assassination threatened the King and his brother.

The Earl of Essex was taken to the Tower on 10 July 1683, and after one day's sojourn in the Lieutenant's Lodgings, was transferred to the house 'on the left hand side of the grassy mound after passing the Bloody Tower Gate', in other words, the residence on Tower Green of Major Hawley, the Gentleman Porter, immediately adjacent to the Lieutenant's Lodgings. With terrible irony, he found himself confined in the very room from which his father, Lord Capel, a prisoner of the Roundheads, had escaped in 1649 but had later been recaptured and beheaded (see my *Great Escapes from the Tower of London*, 1982); moreover the same room had housed Lady Essex's grandfather, the Earl of Northumberland, in Elizabeth's reign and in which he had killed himself. Whether this situation had been deliberately and sadistically planned will never be known, although in the light of subsequent tragic events it may well have been.

On Friday 13 July Lord Russell was taken from the Tower to be tried at the Old Bailey before Judge Jeffries, the Hanging Judge, and on the morning of that day, without previous warning, the Royal Barge arrived at the Tower Wharf and moored at the rarely used King's Steps (still in situ and known as the Queen's Steps), the sudden appearance of the King and Duke of York surprising the sentries on duty there to no small extent, especially as neither of the royal pair had visited the Tower for many years, in fact not since the Coronation. Making their way to Tower Green, they entered the Lieutenant's Lodgings and after spending some time with that officer, Captain Tom Cheek, they re-emerged and, escorted by the Captain, started to walk back towards the Wharf. Meanwhile two schoolboys who lived in Mark Lane, near Tower Hill, having heard of the King's visit and, hoping to see the monarch, had run down to the Tower and made their way to Tower Green; there they, together with a passing manservant, suddenly saw a window in Major Hawley's house open wide – and then a bloodstained razor landed on the ground in front of the building! Next moment, before any of them fully realised what had happened, a maid appeared at the door. 'Murder! Murder!' she screamed and, as they reported later, she snatched up the razor and ran back inside the house.

Attracted by the noise, everyone in the vicinity, soldiers, warders, officials and servants came rushing up; on seeing the commotion, Captain Cheek promptly turned back to ascertain its cause – but oddly enough, neither the King nor James evinced the slightest interest, but continued on their way to the Wharf, where they boarded the Barge and departed.

As the officer in charge, Captain Cheek immediately ordered the crowd to stand back and, entering the house, was faced with a ghastly spectacle, for in a closet adjoining the bedroom the Earl's body lay in a pool of blood; that he was dead was only too apparent, his throat having been cut from ear to ear; indeed so completely that the head was only attached to the torso by a strip of flesh. Looking around for the weapon, the Captain at last saw the razor – lying on the floor some distance away in the bedroom! Shocked at his discovery of the body, he immediately sent for the Tower surgeons, but they could only confirm the obvious. Arthur Capel, Earl of Essex was dead, apparently by his own hand.

The inquest was held in the bedroom the following day, presided over by the Tower coroner. Witnesses were called to attend, statements being obtained from the surgeons, and also from the warders who had guarded the Earl during the short time he had been in the Major's house. The most important witness was Paul Bomeny, the Earl's valet (some prisoners in the Tower were occasionally allowed their own servants, who had to vacate the fortress when the Tower's curfew bell was rung). He gave evidence that on first being confined, the Earl had requested a penknife with which to pare his nails. There had been some delay in granting this, and eventually, on the fatal morning, Essex had persuaded Bomeny to let him have the razor with which the valet shaved him, for the purpose of cutting his nails. Bomeny complied with his master's request, then left to have a conversation with Warder Russell in the corridor.

Shortly afterwards, the Earl's footman arrived with a basket of provisions and gave them to the valet, who then carried it into the bedroom. The room itself was empty, he said in testimony, but he saw that the door to the inner room, the closet, was closed and so naturally assumed that his master was in there. Having no suspicion that anything was untoward, he left the room, but half an hour or so later, on returning, he saw the door was still closed. Puzzled, he called out and, on receiving no reply, summoned the warder; between them they managed to force the door open – to find the Earl in the state previously described.

Warder Russell was questioned, his answers broadly confirming the evidence given by Bomeny, except that he stated that the event

Arthur, Earl of Essex

occurred on the Thursday, not the Friday! This mistake could well have been attributed to nervousness, the warder doubtless worrying that he might well be held responsible in some way for the demise of the prisoner he had been guarding.

The jury brought in a verdict 'that the Earl had died by his own malice' and the mutilated corpse was later interred in St Peter's Chapel, the entry in the deaths register stating 'Arthur, Earl of Essex, cutt his own throat within the Tower, 13 July 1683. Buried within this Chapel'.

Although Lady Essex and other relatives decided to accept the coroner's findings, ugly rumours quickly spread and many questions were raised, questions which pointed the finger of guilt at the very pinnacle of society, none other than the King and his brother. That the Earl had been depressed, there was little doubt; the bizarre history of the room in which he had been imprisoned, the fate of his father, the accusation of treason that he himself faced; yet the very nature of the dreadful wound itself contradicted the possibility of suicide, a wound so savage as to be almost impossible to self-inflict. If he HAD committed suicide, why was the razor not found next to him? It was inconceivable that in his parlous state he could have thrown it into the main room where it was seen by the Lieutenant – and with what motive would he have wished to do that anyway? What of the witnesses, the two boys and the manservant, who swore that they saw the razor flung from the window? And who was the 'maid' who ran out and retrieved it?

Some critics of the day suggested that it was murder, even daring to accuse the two royal brothers and the Lieutenant of being directly responsible; why, that day of all days, did Charles and James choose to visit the Tower? Why, at the time of the discovery of the tragedy, did they not react in the same way as the Lieutenant and return with him to the scene, if only through normal curiosity?

And although common sense decreed that had they wished the death of Essex, they would hardly have attracted suspicion by coming in person, and that they could easily have coerced someone to commit the murder on their behalf, yet some years later a contemporary print showed the Earl being attacked by three well-dressed individuals and even portrayed the body in the position in which it had been found. Nor was that all, for a soldier named Lloyd came forward subsequently and stated that he had been on guard outside Major Hawley's house on that fateful morning, that he had seen two gentlemen enter that residence and not only heard sounds of commotion from an upper room, but had heard someone shout 'My Lord is dead!'. Following this testimony Lloyd found himself in Newgate Prison, but maintained the truth of his statement for the rest of his life. Of course it might well have been that the two men were the footman with the supplies and a companion; the commotion, the breaking down of the door; the shouting, that of Bomeny on finding his dead master, but there were always those believed what they wanted to believe – and anyway, if Lloyd was on duty there at the time, what did he know of the alleged maid who came out and took the razor? Lloyd could consider himself lucky only to suffer imprisonment in Newgate; other dangerous accusations, made by Robert Meek, another sentry, were never taken up by the authorities – or maybe they were, for the soldier's body was later found in the Tower moat, he having apparently drowned. Another amateur detective was one Lawrence Braddon who took it upon himself to investigate the circumstances and indeed questioned Lloyd and the two boys; he disappeared, never to be seen again.

Few of the above contentious and potentially damning questions were reportedly put to the jury; it was after all an inquest and not a trial, and the very fact that these matters were not raised, gave rise to suspicions of it being a cover-up. John Evelyn (1620-1706) the renowned diarist and author, was equally mystified, and said 'This incident exceedingly amaz'd me, My Lord Esssex being so well knowne to me to be a person of such sober and religious deportment, so well at his ease, and so much oblig'd to the King. It is certain that the King and Duke were at the Tower and pass'd by his window about the same time this morning ...... it was wondred by some how it was possible he should do it in the manner he was found, for the wound was so deepe and wide, but more (wondered) that, having passed the jugulars, he should have had strength to proceed so far. There were odd reflections upon it.' Two days later he significantly remarked 'His Majesty is very melancholy.'

But anyway, why would the King want Essex to appear to die by his own hand? A possible reason emerged at the trial of Lord Russell which had started on that memorable day, Friday 13 July. To Judge Jeffries it was patently obvious. If one of three defendants had done away with himself, then it stood to reason (his brand of reasoning) that that was proof he was guilty of being involved in the Plot; *ergo*, it therefore followed that his two colleagues, Lord Russell and Algernon Sidney, were also guilty. Accordingly Jeffries condemned Lord Russell to death, the execution being carried out on 21 July in public on a scaffold built in Lincoln Inn Fields, by the brutally inaccurate Jack Ketch, five blows of the axe being required to complete the decapitation. Algernon Sidney was tried, found guilty and was similarly despatched on 27 December 1683.

So whether Arthur Capel, Earl of Essex died by his own or another's hand, it could be said that it was at least a quicker, more merciful death than that inflicted on his companions in misfortune.

19. The Forefather of Kings,
A Prisoner in The Tower

In the 1420s, during the reign of Henry V of Agincourt fame, the Clerk of the Queen's Wardrobe was a young gentleman of distinguished Welsh stock named Owen Tudor. In his early twenties, extremely tall and handsome, he graced the royal Court, the Queen, Katherine of Valois, daughter of the French King Charles VI, being particular taken by his elegant charm. Henry V died in 1422, the immature and ill-fated Henry VI succeeding to the throne, and after the customary mourning period had ended, the Court resumed its normal round of gaiety and festivities. During one of these light-hearted dances attended by the Queen and her ladies in waiting, Owen, in attempting too elaborate a pirouette, overbalanced and fell, finishing up with his head in the royal lap. This intimate, albeit accidental encounter, was instrumental in furthering a close personal relationship between them despite the ladies of the Court diplomatically chiding her 'for lowering herself in paying any attention to a person who, though possessing some personal accomplishments and advantages, yet had no princely or even gentle alliance but belonged to a barbarous class of savages inferior to the lowest English yeoman'. At such *lese majeste* the Queen retorted that 'being a Frenchwoman she had not been aware that there was any difference of race in the British island!'. And, no-one daring to interfere further, their friendship proceeded to develop into what must surely be one of the great romances of all time, a love affair which had unexpectedly historic and also tragic consequences.

During their years together, Katherine bore her lover three children and it is believed that they eventually married in secret in 1435. But disaster was to shatter their idyll. Henry VI being too young to rule, Humphrey, Duke of Gloucester had been appointed Regent, and on discovering the liaison he angrily threatened that anyone 'who should dare to marry a Queen-Dowager or any lady holding lands of the Crown, without the consent of the King and Council' would suffer severest penalties. Voluntarily or not, the

Queen retired into retreat in Bermondsey Abbey in 1436 and sadly died on 3 January 1437 at the age of thirty-six. Owen Tudor, despite seeking sanctuary in Westminster Abbey, was eventually induced to give himself up and was incarcerated in Newgate Prison. But that gaol could not hold him, for he managed to escape, an anonymous manuscript describing how 'one oweyn, no man of birthe neither of livelihood, brak out of Newgate at night at serchynge tyme through help of his priest and wente his way, hurtynge foule his keeper, but at the last blessyd by God he was taken agane, the whiche Oweyn hadd prevylie wedded the quene Katherine and had ii or iii chyldren by her, unwetying (unknown to) the commin people tyl that she were dyed and buryed'. One prison that could and did hold him was of course, the Tower of London, where he was confined in 1438 for several months.

Upon Henry VI reaching maturity and asserting his authority, he not only ordered the release of Owen (who was after all, his stepfather!) but granted him an annuity, further appointing him King's Lieutenant of Denbighland, together with all its rents and profits, in 1460. But Owen's good fortune was not to last very long, for by 1461 he had joined the Lancastrians in the War of the Roses and at the Battle of Mortimer's Cross was taken prisoner. As one of the most prominent captives, he was escorted under strong guard to Hereford and sentenced to death. Little time was wasted in carrying out the sentence and at the market cross in that town, he faced the executioner. To the very end he believed that he would be reprieved, a contemporary chronicler stating that 'he waved all away and trusted he would not be beheaded until he saw the axe and the block, and he still trusted on pardon and grace till the collar of his red velvet doublet was ripped away. Then he said 'This head shall lie on the block that was wont to lie on Queen Katherine's lap' and so meekly took his death'.

The mangled remains were buried within the Church of Grey Friars in Hereford, and on 24 October 1933 workmen digging a drainage trench on the site of that long-demolished church discovered three skeletons buried three feet down in the ground. One skeleton was that of a man six feet two inches tall and it was decided that in all probability it was that of Owen Tudor. After a brief ceremony, the remains were decently re-interred nearby.

Why Owen Tudor was imprisoned in the Tower is a mystery, for he had broken no law, yet it was common knowledge that he had enemies, among whom was the Regent, Humphrey, Duke of Gloucester, a man who possibly feared a challenge to his authority should Owen, being the King's stepfather, claim to replace him as regent. Had the Duke contrived to bring about Owen's execution on some trumped-up charge, the historic consequences would have been momentous, to say the least, for Owen Tudor was the founder of the Tudor dynasty. His eldest son by Katherine of Valois became Earl of Richmond, father of King Henry VII, the royal line continuing through Henry VIII and Queens Mary and Elizabeth. And while one might not consider these monarchs to have had pleasant personalities or benevolent natures, their overwhelming influence on English history from 1485 to 1603 is indisputable.

To end on a bizarre note; After Queen Katherine's death in 1437 her remains were placed in the Lady Chapel in Westminster Abbey. The coffin was partially wrapped in a sheet of lead taken from the roof and, the lid not having been replaced, her body lay exposed from the waist upwards and one of the tourist 'attractions' of the Abbey was to see and touch her parched corpse. Described by the historian Dart as 'continuing to be seen, the bones firmly united and thinly covered with flesh, like scrapings of fine leather' it remained like that for many generations and was visited by Samuel Pepys, who wrote in his Diary that 'On Shrove Tuesday 1669 I to the Abbey went, and by favour did see the body of Queen Katherine of Valois, and had the upper part of her body in my hands, and I did kiss her mouth, reflecting that I did kiss a queen, and this my birthday and I thirty-six years old and I did kiss a Queen!' A boastful comment, surely verging on necrophilia, the cadaver being two hundred and thirty two years old. Regrettably it was not until 1776 that decency prevailed and Queen Katherine, wife of the ex-prisoner in the Tower Owen Tudor, progenitors of Tudor kings and queens, was finally buried in the vaults of the Abbey.

20. A Miscellany of Minor Mysteries

A Message from Beyond

A tablet on the west wall of the Chapel Royal of St Peter ad Vincula is inscribed;

'Col. John Gurwood, CB, Deputy Lieut, 1839 - 43, died 27 Dec 1845, aged 57, buried 3 January 1846' and at the foot of the tablet is placed a marble replica of two volumes of the Duke of Wellington's despatches which he helped to compile. This brave soldier was severely wounded in the head while leading a charge against overwhelming numbers of the enemy at the storming of Cuidad Rodrigo in Spain during the campaign against Napoleon and was later appointed to the post mentioned above.

More than forty years after he died, in June 1889, a curious incident occurred at a seance. The spiritualist found herself writing on the planchette (a heart-shaped board on wheels with a pencil attached, that writes words apparently guided by a spirit) the name 'John Gurwood' followed by the words ' I killed myself forty-four years ago next Xmas.' Asked if he was in the army, the answer given was 'Yes but it was the pen, not the sword that did for me.' Questioned as to where he was wounded, the spiritualist found herself writing 'In the Peninsula in the head, I was wounded in 1810.' Then followed a rough outline of what was later discovered to be the Gurwood crest, a grant of arms by the King for bravery in the field, the design being that of a mural coronet with a castle in the centre, from which stretched an arm holding a scimitar.

The baffling aspect was that the spiritualist had not only never heard of John Gurwood but knew nothing of his crest. Even had she visited the Tower and seen the tablet, there was, quite rightly, nothing on it to indicate that the Colonel had committed suicide. Even more incomprehensible was the fact that the writing and the sketch were upside down to the medium, as if her hand was being directed by the unseen being sitting on the opposite side of the table to her.

The reference to having been killed by the pen could well have referred to his part in the writing of Wellington's despatches, having previously sustained wounds to the head, but the motive or reason for the message was never established, nor did it ever recur, but one can only feel a great sense of pity on studying the tablet, placed as it is in a Chapel which contains the remains of three executed Queens of England and many others who similarly suffered.

Who was the Unknown Subaltern?

In 1916 a young army officer was escorted into the Tower and confined in comfortably furnished quarters in the East Casemates (the apartments within the thickness of the outer wall), having been charged with offences relating to the passing of cheques for which he had insufficient funds in his account. Observing the momentary inattention of the sentry on guard outside his quarter one day, he seized the opportunity and coolly walked out, receiving and acknowledging salutes from the soldiers on duty at the main gate.

Boarding a train at Mark Lane tube station (as it was then) on Tower Hill, he travelled to the West End and entered a restaurant, where he enjoyed an excellent meal – paying for it with yet another 'rubber' cheque! Pleasantly replete, and perhaps feeling a certain amount of remorse at the military action which would inevitably be taken against those who should have ensured his continued confinement, he made his way back to the Tower. There, he observed that the alarm had been raised and in the controlled melee that was taking place he calmly returned to his quarter. It was said that at his eventual court martial, his little escapade was viewed but lightly – although one wonders not only who he was – but what was the fate of the unfortunate sentry?

A Tower Escape that led to Westminster Abbey Sacrilege

Of the relatively small number of escapes from the Tower, perhaps the one which had such devastating and unforeseen consequences was that of two men, Robert Hawle and John Shackle in 1378. They were knights in the army led by the Black Prince during his campaign in the north of Spain, and during the Battle of Najara they had captured the Count of Dene and brought him back to this country. It was a common and lucrative practice in those days to take hostage a prosperous member of the enemy and keep him captive, for years if necessary, until a ransom was forthcoming.

The Count said it was necessary that he be allowed to return to Spain in order to raise the large sum demanded and so the two knights agreed to let him go, having first insisted that he left his son in their hands as surety. Accordingly the Spanish Count departed but, *en route*, collapsed and died. The two knights, loth to see a small fortune slip out of their grasp, refused to release the Count's son, and their ploy could have worked had not their captive had a powerful friend at Court, none other than John of Gaunt, Duke of Lancaster, son of Edward III, a man not to be trifled with. Having married Constance, daughter of Pedro the Cruel, and assumed the title of King of Castile, he was in some sympathy with the Spanish royalty's resentment at the knights' unrelenting attitude and, as it would seem that they were unwilling to divulge the whereabouts of their captive, John of Gaunt used his influence to have them thrown into the Tower.

How they managed to escape is a mystery to this day, but escape they did, and no doubt those responsible for guarding them adequately, suffered dire punishment. The alarm was immediately raised and, the men being seen running up Tower Hill, they were hotly pursued by Alan Buxhill, Constable of the Tower, Sir Ralph Ferrers and fifty armed men of the Tower garrison. The two men headed for Westminster, and desperately seeking sanctuary, fled into the Abbey, penetrating as far as the Choir. At the time High Mass was being celebrated, it being 11 August, the Festival of St Taurinus, but as the sound of running feet and the shouts of their pursuers echoed from the hallowed walls, the service broke up in utter confusion. The knight Shackle managed to elude the armed party, doubtless via a side door, but Robert Hawle was intercepted. Twice he fled round the Choir, the soldiers hacking at him as he ran, until at length, having sustained a dozen wounds from their swords, he fell dead in front of the Prior's Stall at the north side of the entrance to the Choir.

The ancient Abbey having been so severely desecrated, Shackle was regarded as a martyr and given the honour, at that time very unusual, of burial within the walls – the first, it is believed, to be interred in the South Transept, to be followed a few years later by Chaucer, who was buried at his feet. A brass effigy and a long epitaph marked the stone where the body of the knight was interred and another inscription was engraved where he fell and on which his effigy may still be traced.

The repercussions were considerable, for not only was the Abbey closed for four months but Parliament itself was suspended lest the members of its assembly be polluted by sitting within its desecrated precincts. The whole shocking case was heard in the presence of the King, Richard II, the Abbot, William of Colchester, together with the Archbishops and Bishops, agreeing that nothing less than the excommunication of the Constable and Sir Ralph Ferrers would suffice. Not only was this repeated publicly every Wednesday and Friday by the Bishop of London in St Paul's Cathedral but both sacriligious offenders had to pay the then large sum of £200 to the Abbey as penance.

Following the murder of his confederate, John Shackle, no longer a fugitive, agreed to release his Spanish prisoner (who had been acting as his valet) in exchange for 500 marks down-payment and 100 marks annually for life. On his death, he too was buried in a grave in the Abbey, near to that of his companion.

At the Abbey the whole question of entitlement to sanctuary was reviewed, it being decided by the ecclesiastical authorities that it should not be exercised or available to debtors. In all, a sorry and lamentable tale, one which need never have happened had Hawle and Shackle not managed to escape from the Tower under such mysterious circumstances.

Who Stole Parts of the Dead Bodies?

One would naturally assume that at the time of burial within the Chapel Royal, the bodies of even the most proven guilty of victims would nevertheless be treated with the utmost reverence and respect for human decency. Admittedly, the head of Saint Thomas More was displayed on London Bridge in accordance with the judgment passed at his trial, it later being claimed by his daughter Meg Roper from the watchman and at her death was put in a leaden box somewhat in the shape of a beehive, open in the front, which was then placed in a niche within the family tomb in St Dunstan's Church in Canterbury. The vault was accidently broken into in 1835 when reportedly it was discovered that the lower jaw had been stolen. An iron grill was then affixed in the stonework surrounding the niche to deter further vandalism.

His torso was interred in the Chapel Royal, next to that of Archbishop Fisher, another victim of the headsman, but even in that hallowed spot, parts of his body were taken away as holy relics. But who sanctioned the removal of the bloodstained vertebra of his neck which, as reported by Dom Bede Camm in his book *Forgotten Shrines* (pub 1900), is revered by the English Canonesses at Bruges in Belgium? How did someone originally obtain the tooth and a piece of one of his bones which, according to the same source, are now at Stonyhurst College?

Similarly with the remains of Bl. Margaret Pole, Countess of Salisbury. Condemned to death by Henry VIII, on 27 May 1541 she was brutally put to the axe on Tower Green 'the regular executioners being busy in the North, a wretched and blundering youth had been chosen to take his place, who literally hacked off her head and shoulders to pieces in the most pitiful manner'. Her mangled remains were taken into the Chapel Royal, yet before she was buried, some person extracted her thigh bone! The motive for this is not known, for no mention of it being revered in any of the Catholic institutions is recorded, but where was it kept, and by whom, until it 'was shown as a curiosity to the King of Siam during his visit to the Tower' centuries later?

The identities of some people who were buried in the Chapel Royal of St Peter during the Middle Ages, have never been established other than by the cryptic entries in the ancient burial registers. As such an entry confirms that a burial actually took place, one man in particular must somewhere have been deprived of, not just a body part, but his entire corpse, for only his internal organs are recorded as being interred! Under the period headed 1557-1565 appears the entry 'Lo. Wardens bewells buried in ye Chapell', yet no trace can be found of any lord ('Lo' being the standard abbreviation at that time) whose remains were, for whatever reason, buried elsewhere bereft of his bowels.

Although it was the custom in earlier centuries for the internal organs of members of the royal family to be deposited separately in caskets which were then placed either on or at the foot of their coffins in Westminster Abbey, and also for the hearts of some kings to be interred in foreign cities (Richard I's heart being revered in Rouen Cathedral and his body buried in the great Angevin Abbey of Fontevrault with his ancestors, for instance) our Lo. Warden would hardly seem to be of that rank and privilege, and anyway had he been so, the whereabouts of his corpse would also have been recorded.

The rank of 'Warden' could have been a title denoting a barony, but the *Complete Peerage* contains no allusion to any such title. That there were Wardens is not disputed, there being such appointments as 'Warden of the Cinque Ports' and 'Warden of Dover Castle', yet the many chronicles and reference works about the City's notables and personalities fail to throw any light on the owner of the bowels buried in such royal surroundings. Truly a mystery unsolved and probably unsolveable.

But if the whereabouts of Lo. Warden's remains are a puzzle, what of the quandary posed by the contents of the splendid alabaster tomb of Sir Richard Cholmondeley and his wife which graces the centre of the Chapel Royal? Are their remains contained therein or not? And why is their tomb here anyway? For that we must go back to the year 1513, to the reign of Henry VII, when Richard Cholmondeley was knighted for his valour at the battle of Flodden Field and appointed Lieutenant of the Tower. It could hardly be said that he excelled at the job, or that he had an equable nature, for when a riot broke out in the City during his term of office, he didn't parley with the ringleaders or send his garrison troops in – instead he ordered the cannon positioned along the northern battlemented walls of the Tower to open fire or, as Hall recounted in his *Chronicles* 'Whilst this ruffling continued, Syr Richard Chomly, Knight, Lieutenant of the Tower, no great friende of the citie, in a frantyke fury losed certayn pieces of ordinance, and shot into the citie; whiche did little harme, howbeit his good will apeered'.

While occupying that post he had the tomb built in readiness for his ultimate demise, a not uncommon practice in those days; so ready was it in fact, that on the catafalque appear in Latin the words

'*Jacent Corpora Ricardi Cholmondeley militis et dna (domina) Elizabeth consortis sue qui suis…obiit…di… mensi……………quorum animabus Deus propietur, Amen*'

Translated, that reads 'Here lies the bodies of Richard Cholmondeley soldier and Lady Elizabeth his wife who died respectively on….day of the month of……………… whose souls are in God's keeping, Amen'

(It has been said, true or not, that the fact his effigy lies with the legs lying straight proves that he did not intend to get involved in any

The Chapel Royal of St Peter ad Vincula

future military activity, for the legs of effigies of those who did die on the battlefield were sculptured with their legs crossed). He certainly did not occupy the tomb while still in post, for he retired in 1534. Nor was he buried in it when he died in 1544, for the entry of his interment does not appear until listed in the 1554-1557 burial register which states 'Sir Roger Chomleis ffather buried in the Chapell'.

Sir Richard and his wife Elizabeth had no children but it was common knowledge that he was the natural father of Sir Roger Chomley (who chose to spell his name that way). That young man later became Lord Chief Justice and was one of those who witnessed Edward VI's will which declared Lady Jane Grey to be Queen, rather than Mary Tudor. And when Mary ousted Jane from the throne, she took her revenge in 1553 by having Roger Chomley confined in the Tower, a large fine having to be paid to secure his release. And if, as is highly likely, he saw his father's tomb in the Chapel, what more natural would it have been for him than to have his father's remains transferred from where-ever they had been buried, together with possibly those of Lady Elizabeth, to that tomb? And that it did happen, is confirmed, as stated above, by the 1554-1557 entry in the register. But why were the date and month details on the catafalque not completed? Or were they, only to be later chipped away, the level of the stone there being lower than the surrounding alabaster. But why?

At this point the story takes a strange twist. During the Civil War, when victory of the Commonwealth forces appeared certain, the priest of the Chapel must have had the foreboding that any of the Chapel's religious symbols not conforming with Cromwell's Puritan ideals would be desecrated and destroyed (as indeed they were, together with the Regalia and Jewels). Determined to thwart the Roundheads as far as the Chapel's baptismal font was concerned (which, experts now believe, dates back to the reign of Edward III in the fourteenth century) he decided that the lesser of two evils was preferable and so broke up the font himself – and concealed the large fragments in the tomb, causing a certain amount of damage to the stonework as he did so. In choosing that as a hiding place, not only was the precious font successfully concealed from the Roundheads, but the secret of its whereabouts died with the priest, for he died or was killed before the end of the war.

During the next two hundred years or so the tomb was moved to different places in the Chapel until in 1876 Queen Victoria gave

Monument of Sir Richard Cholmondeley and his Wife in St Peter's Chapel.

permission for a complete restoration of the interior of the building to be carried out. And when the tomb was opened, the font was discovered, carefully reassembled and is now used for its original purpose. But of the bodies there was no sign, just a lot of dust. But was it dust? Had the crushing impact of the chunks of broken font caused the skeleton(s) to disintegrate, the air entering when the priest had forced an opening adding to the deterioration of the shattered remains? The moving of the tomb to various positions would further have exacerbated the condition of the contents. So is it merely dust that still remains within the tomb – or is it the powdered human remains of Sir Richard and his wife Elizabeth?

The Constable of the Tower who became a Highwayman

The only mystery here is how on earth Geoffrey de Mandeville could ever have been appointed to the prestigious post of Constable of His Majesty's Royal Palace and Fortress the Tower of London in the first place! Admittedly his father William had been Constable, as had his grandfather, also named Geoffrey, a fearless Norman knight who had landed with the armies of William the Conqueror, he having had the distinction of being the first Constable to command the castle when the White Tower was built in 1078, but the family qualities must have deteriorated considerably by the time the third generation came along.

In the year 1140 our Geoffrey took up post enthusiastically and full of determination to better himself; indeed so ambitious was he that eventually he was created Earl of Essex. Whether it was boredom with the job or the realisation that further ennoblement was beyond his reach will never be known. Suffice it to say that at the end of thirteen years he resigned – and became a highwayman! He also sided with King Stephen's opponents, and it was while he was embroiled in a skirmish with government troops at Middleham in Suffolk that he was mortally wounded.

His burial proved to be an insoluble problem, for having been previously excommunicated by the Pope for acts of sacrilege and the seriousness of the crimes he had committed, no priest would commit him to the grave. Yet to leave the body where it had fallen would only attract the ravens and other of nature's scavengers. At length the Knights Templars, for whom Geoffrey had rendered some slight service in the past, came to the rescue. Shrouding his corpse in one of the habits of their Order, they brought it to the Temple, near where now is London's Embankment. There, encased in a leaden coffin, it was suspended between two stout trees in the garden.

One hesitates to affirm that it swung there in the breeze for any length of time, but it was not until twenty years later that on appeal, a later Pope lifted the ban on his burial, and so the remains of Geoffrey de Mandeville, Earl of Essex, were 'buried in front of the West Door of the Temple Church' and his effigy, clad as a Knight Templar, reclines therein.

Thomas Norton, Rackmaster and Prisoner

In Queen Elizabeth's reign the Tower's rack seldom stood idle. This fearsome device was not, as many think, an instrument of punishment as such; on the contrary it was a machine specifically designed to persuade someone, man or woman, whom the authorities had already decided was guilty, to confess first that they were indeed guilty and, as there was little point in executing one conspirator if others remained at large, coerce them to divulge the names of any accomplices. Or, as Sir Francis Walsingham, Elizabeth's Secretary of State, wrote on 27 March 1582 'None was put to the rack that was not at first by some manifest evidence known to the Council to be

NE OF THE INSTRUMENTS OF TORTURE, CALLED " THE SCAVENGER'S DAUGHTER,'
EMPLOYED IN THE TOWER OF LONDON ON THE 10TH DECEMBER, 1580.

guilty of treason, so that it was well assured beforehand that there was
no innocent tormented. Also none was tormented to know whether
he was guilty or no, but for the Queen's safety to know the manner of
the treason and the accomplices'.

Early models of the rack consisted of a rectangular open frame,
like a bedstead, over six feet in length, standing on four legs, about
three feet high. The prisoner was laid on his back on the floor,
having his wrists and ankles tied to a windlass at each corner of the
frame, these being operated by levers turned in opposite directions,
thereby hoisting the victim until almost level with the frame. The
strain and unbearable agony of being so lifted can well be imagined,
nor did the pain end there, for unless a confession was forthcoming,
the levers continued to turn, the ropes continued to creak, until
wrists and ankles, hips and shoulder blades were dislocated, sinews
and ligaments torn, muscles twisted beyond redemption.

A later version incorporated a rachet mechanism operated by
only two men, this eventually being replaced by a rack having a
central wooden roller, a rachet at each end fitted with a control bar
which could be operated by one man – and in Elizabeth's reign, that
man was Thomas Norton, Rackmaster of the Tower.

He was of course assisted by the author's predecessors, the yeoman warders, as evidenced by State Papers of 1583 which stated 'The Queen's servants, the warders, whose office and act it is to handle the rack, were ever by those that attended the examinations, specially charged to use it in as charitable a manner as such a thing might be'. But how could you rack someone 'charitably'?

First of all, psychological coercion was applied, the prisoner being led down into the shadowy dungeon of the White Tower where, illuminated by the feebly flickering brands in their wall brackets, he would be shown the rack and other similar machines. He or she would then be 'invited' to confess, only the very strong willed or highly principled refusing to avail themselves of the opportunity.

The completely innocent would of course find their protestations totally ignored and would be racked until they confessed to crimes they had never committed; anything, even execution, was preferable to being virtually torn asunder on the dreaded rack.

Many were those who suffered. Edward Peacham 'was this day racked before torture, in torture, between torture and after torture'. Nicholls and Pitt 'were to be brought to the rack and to feel the smart thereof, if their examiners shall think good, for the better boulting out of the truth of the matter'. Bannister and Barker were 'to be put to the rack and find the taste thereof' but after the 'taste' the Commissioner examining them reported 'I suppose we have gotten so mych at this time as is lyke to be had; yet tomorrow we do intend to bring them to the rack, not in any hope to get any thyng worthy of that payne or feare, but because it is earnestly commanded unto us'.

Thomas Norton, Rackmaster, servant of the Queen and the State, was in duty bound to obey, and yet it was reported that in 1583 he expressed his dissatisfaction with the established church and was imprisoned in the Tower. Knowing the hideous, excruciating agony caused by the instrument he operated and equally aware that no offender was exempt from its persuasive ways, it was almost beyond the bounds of credibility that he should even contemplate doing such a thing. Perhaps he had inadvertently sympathised with a sufferer or commented casually on the unusual severity of one particular session; the reporting of such an off-the-bloodstained-cuff remark by rivals or enemies in those days of intrigue and conspiracy would have been enough to bring down a charge of treason on his head, with the inevitable results. However, Thomas Norton was fortunate, for his incarceration was of short duration, whether because he was proved innocent, or whether no substitute of equivalent experience could be found, is not known. Upon his release he continued his racking career in the White Tower dungeon for a few months until, on 10 March 1584 he died in his home in Sharpenhoe, Bedfordshire, and was buried in the church of the nearby village of Streatley.

Who Slew the Yeoman Warder?

Literally thousands of tourists visit the Tower each day, some of them having more interesting lives than others, and so it was a pleasure, while on duty one day in March 1981, when the author met a Dr David Scott. No ordinary doctor, but an astronaut, not only having been a member of the crew in Gemini VIII, Apollo IX and XV, but one of the men who had actually walked on the moon. Entertaining him and his charming wife in our apartment that evening, we discussed his space flights and I pointed out to him that some of the early and primitive maps of the heavens which, over the centuries, had developed out of all recognition into those eventually used for his momentous journeys, originated in the Tower of London! They were in fact drawn by an 'astronomical observator', John Flamsteed, who was appointed by Charles II to observe and plot the movements of the moon and the stars from his eyrie in the round turret of the White Tower.

The fact that I, as a yeoman warder, was present in the Tower of London at the same time as was David Scott, a man who had walked on the moon, has an uncanny parallel in circumstances which occurred three hundred years earlier when, in 1675, John Flamsteed, the Astronomer Royal, was working on his charts in the round turret at the same time as a Yeoman Warder Halley was doubtless on duty elsewhere in the grounds of the Tower.

Edmond Halley joined the Body of Yeoman Warders on 14 September 1664 in the days when the qualifications for becoming a yeoman warder were not restricted solely to those having had military experience, and indeed many warders retained and at times actively pursued their civilian jobs. Edmond was not only a salter and soap boiler, but also owned several houses in the City, together with the Dog Tavern, a hostelry conveniently situated just up the road from the Tower in Billingsgate! He had married Ann Robinson and, while living at Haggerston, two or so miles north of his place of work, she gave birth to a child on 8 November 1656, a boy whom they also christened Edmond. Halley Senior was not highly educated, and no doubt it came as a great surprise to him and his wife when their son showed all the signs of being a near-genius. First attending St Paul's School, by the age of seventeen he was a student at Queen's College, Oxford, and qualified as a mathematician, with strong leanings towards astrology.

After graduating, Halley Junior travelled extensively around the Continent, studying the effects of trade winds and monsoons, surveying coasts and tides, but his first love was unlocking the secrets of the heavens and analysing the orbits of the planets. One of his greatest achievements was to forecast the total solar eclipse of 1715, and six years after that, in 1721, he became Astronomer Royal. However all his previous discoveries were themselves eclipsed by his predictions regarding a certain astronomical event, one so remarkably accurate, that the celestial body itself which passes the Earth at regular intervals was forthwith known as 'Halley's Comet'!

Alas, his father, the yeoman warder of the Tower of London, did not live long enough to bask in the fame of his talented son. On 5 March 1683 he left his house as usual, it being assumed he was going to work, but he was never seen again until, five weeks later, on 12 April, his lifeless body was found in a field in the parish of Stroud, near Rochester in Kent.

Although rumours circulated that he had been worried over the debts incurred by his ownership of the Dog Tavern and therefore might have committed suicide, the jury at the inquest brought in a verdict of murder. Regrettably details of any injuries he might have sustained were not recorded, and his possible assailant was never traced. Death by natural causes was ruled out, he being in perfect health, and as far as was known he had no business rivals who would go to those extreme lengths. His funeral took place at Barking, Essex, in the church in which his parents had been married, and he was interred in the cemetery there, near their graves and close to that of his wife.

So how did he die? Was he ambushed by a footpad and resisted? Slain in an attempt to fight off a cutpurse? Confronted by a highwayman and refused to hand over his valuables? We will never know.

Halley's Comet?

21. Mystical Miasma

The Spectre of the Spiral Stairway

'Whatever married man did not repent of his marriage, or quarrel in a year and a day after it, should go to his Priory and demand the promised flitch of bacon, on his swearing to the truth, kneeling on two stones in the church-yard'. That ancient tradition, still practised albeit rarely, dates back to the thirteenth century and was instituted by Lord Robert Fitzwalter. The prize was known as the Dunmow Flitch, the Priory in question being Dunmow Priory, situated in the Essex town of that name. Robert Fitzwalter was Lord of Dunmow, although he spent much of his time at his London address, Baynard's Castle, in Surrey, now long since demolished. However one can be quite certain that he would not have considered his Sovereign, King John, to be eligible for such a philanthropic award, for John, although married to Queen Isabella of Angouleme, harboured lustful thoughts directed towards a beautiful damsel called Maud, or Matilda, the Fair – for she happened to be Fitzwalter's daughter!

The King's improper advances were spurned by that young lady, but so determined was the monarch that in the year 1212 he had her kidnapped from the family home in Dunmow and brought to the Tower of London, where she was imprisoned in the round turret of the White Tower. On hearing of the dastardly deed, her outraged father sought to raise the other barons in revolt against the monarch, but failing in his efforts, he was forced to flee to France, his estates then being forfeited to the Crown.

As the months went by, John continued to force his unwanted attentions on Maud, but she refused to speak to him or even the courtiers who conveyed his ardent pleas. Eventually, determined that if he could not have her, no-one else should, he arranged that her food should include a poisoned egg and Maud, unsuspecting his murderous intent, ate it and died. Her body was taken back to Dunmow and interred in the family vault there.

When the news of her murder reached France, Lord Fitzwalter returned to England, to find that the barons were now on the brink of rising up against King John and Robert, placing himself at their head, was thereby instrumental in forcing the King to sign (actually to make his mark) on the Magna Carta at Runnymeade. So it could be said that the Charter which gave us all our civic freedom originated with a poisoned egg eaten in the White Tower by Maud the Fair!

But does her spirit still haunt that ancient building? One afternoon in 1980 a London Tourist Board guide, conducting a party through the White Tower, reported that he had distinctly felt a hand grasp his shoulder and squeeze it twice. Assuming it was a tourist seeking his attention, he turned round immediately – to find no-one there, the members of his group being some yards away!

One man who actually did see 'someone' was an Armouries warden who, at five minutes past eight one morning in 1978, long before any visitors were admitted, was sweeping the floor in one of the rooms. As he was thus engaged he happened to look up and saw, through one of the glass display cases, a woman. Puzzled at her presence, he walked round the cabinet and saw her move through an archway and round the corner into the next room. On following her he saw that there was no-one there, and as the only way out was up the spiral stairs, he ascended them, only to find that the door at the top, leading into the Chapel Royal of St John, was locked and bolted. Summoning his colleagues, the whole area was searched, but no sign of the woman was ever found.

That episode, occurring as it did, in broad daylight, must have been disturbing enough, but the incident experienced by a night security guard on duty in the White Tower at 11.15 pm one night in September 1980 was enough to make his pulses race faster than usual, as he admitted to me when, on the following day, he described what happened. He had entered via an upper storey and then approached the spiral stairway which connects the various floors. As he started to go down he suddenly became aware, out of the corner of his eye, of a woman going up. She seemed to be leaning forward as she mounted the stairs, for the upper half of her body was obscured by the newel post, the thick stone centre pillar of the stairway, but he recalled that she was wearing a long black and grey skirt of some kind. Before he had really comprehended exactly what he had seen, he had taken a further two steps downwards, so he immediately turned back and ascended. Climbing as quickly as he could, his adrenalin flowing, and trying to see round each bend in the stairs before reaching there, eventually he reached the top – to find himself facing a locked door! He confessed afterwards that although completely mystified, he was relieved that the apparition had not turned round and come down again to meet him!

So could it have been the ghost of the young girl, so brutally murdered for refusing to yield to the King, who one morning had alarmed the warden sweeping the floor? Was it her hand that had touched the guide's shoulder? Could it really have been Maud the Fair who in the dead of night was seen mounting the spiral stairs? It may have been – for beyond that locked door was the round turret!

The Stone-Throwing Ghost

Joining the Wakefield and the Lanthorn Towers on the south side of the Fortress is a forty-foot high crenellated wall approximately six feet wide, and access to the top of it can only be gained via the doorways in each of the two towers. At about 8.30 pm on the moonless night of 19 October 1978 the sentry patrolling between the inner and outer walls in that area suddenly became aware of small stones hitting his legs and boots. The security lights were on, and there was no-one in the vicinity. He continued his patrol, only to experience further stones, thrown singly, striking his legs. Mystified – and doubtless hoping to avoid further scratches on his highly polished boots! – he called to his colleague on the adjoining beat and asked him to change over; on doing so, he too was peppered with small stones. At that, the men decided to call out the guard and on their arrival, as usual, the area was scrupulously searched, with negative results. There was no wind whatsoever, so the stones could not have been blown from the top of the inner wall, the direction from which the stones came; the doors at both ends of the wall-walk were not only bolted and secured but also had additional barred gates locked across them. On inspecting the wall-walk nothing could be found to arouse suspicion and the dust on it lay undisturbed.

Even more baffling was the fact that the trajectory of the stones was such that no-one standing on the other side of the wall could possibly have thrown the stones to clear the top of the wall and score hits so accurately on a moving target. Nor could anyone have stood there without being seen by the night security guard whose office was situated on the ground floor of the Lanthorn Tower on that side of the wall.

The author, going on duty nearby at 6.15 am the following morning was not only given a full account of the night's events, but was also given three of the flinty missiles – and holding them in my hand, I sometimes wonder who – or what – held them before they struck the sentry's legs – perhaps a Tudor poltergeist?!

If so it could well have been the same one who, two years later, caused annoyance, if not minor havoc, in the Lanthorn security office, members of the staff repeatedly finding the electric kettle switched on when it had been switched off, and the refrigerator switched off when left on! Consequently, in order to thwart the spectral prankster, the kettle was always unplugged from the socket when not in use but, it being necessary to keep the refrigerator running all the time, the wall switch was taped over. But there was no frustrating the phantom fingers, for the switch was still occasionally being found in the 'off' position, the food thawing and the cold drinks tepid!

The Red-Haired Lady on the Queen's House Stairs

The Queen's House, a magnificent Tudor building in the south-west corner of Tower Green, rich in timbered panels and ceilings, steeped in tradition, was built in 1530 on the orders of Henry VIII. He intended to live there as an alternative to the White Tower but having disposed of Cardinal Wolsey (who was heading for the block and a beheading, but fortuitously died *en route*) the King commandeered Hampton Court and so the new house became the official residence of the Lieutenant of the Tower, it being known as the Lieutenant's Lodgings. In 1880 it was renamed the Queen's House, in which the Resident Governor and his family live.

It was there in bygone days that prisoners brought to the Tower were initially questioned, 'booked in' and assigned their various quarters in the fortress. Some, Guy Fawkes, Anne Askew and others were brought from their prison quarters to be interrogated there, but the really important prisoners were actually confined either there or in the Bell Tower which backs on to it, a tower which can only be entered via the Queen's House, all thereby being under the day-to-day supervision of the Lieutenant. Those who endured imprisonment in those two buildings read like a veritable list from history; Princess Elizabeth (later Elizabeth I), Anne Boleyn,

Katherine Howard, Sir Thomas More, Archbishop Fisher and many others. Lady Margaret Douglas, Countess of Lennox was imprisoned there for five years on three different occasions, Lady Arabella Stuart endured over four years confinement only to die, her sanity gone. The doomed Lady Jane Grey was accomodated there for a short while and in more recent centuries the Quaker William Penn, founder of Pennsylvania, and Rudolph Hess, Deputy Fuhrer of Nazi Germany also found themselves deprived of their freedom behind those timbered walls.

So it is hardly surprising that their suffering and deprivation has given rise to the many instances of supernatural occurrences reported over the last two centuries, accounts of ghostly footsteps (see my *Beefeaters of the Tower of London* pub. 1985), the unnatural coldness in some of the rooms, the inexplicable sounds heard, even ghostly sightings. And it could have been one of the latter which was experienced by a secretary one dark evening in April 1994. She was alone in the building and, needing some papers from an upper room, started to ascend the main stairway. As she did so, she looked up – to see a woman facing her, a motionless figure who, in her own words, existed only 'from the waist up, as if in a portrait'. Caught completely unawares, she later recalled the appearance of the figure, noting the white collar and the fact that 'she' had red hair. In such a situation it is noteworthy that all sense of time usually deserts the witness, and this level-headed young lady was no exception, describing afterwards how time seemed to stand still, until the apparition suddenly vanished. Unbelieving, she automatically continued to mount the stairs, and quite some time elapsed before she was able to recover from the shock.

Who could the ghostly figure have been? The most likely name to spring to mind is of course Princess Elizabeth who, like most of the Tudors, had red hair, and the 'white collar' could have been the ruff, which she made fashionable and therefore mandatory in Court circles. Admittedly she was not executed, but at the time of her imprisonment, under suspicion of being involved in some of treasonable plots prevailing at that time, her mind must have been in an agonised state of constant turmoil lest her half-sister Queen Mary should suddenly decide that such threats to her throne could be eliminated only by condemning her to follow in the footsteps of her mother Anne Boleyn, up the scaffold steps on Tower Green.

SELECT BIBLIOGRAPHY

Annales of England J Stow 1580
Calendar of State Papers, Domestic Series
Chapel in the Tower, D.C. Bell 1877
Chronicle E. Hall 1809
Chronicles R. Holinshed 1808
Chronicles & Annals J. Stow 1580-1605
Colonial Entry Book
Crowns and Coronations W Jones 1898
Diary, J. Evelyn ed. 1850
Diary, S. Pepys 1893
Forgotten Shrines Dom Bede Camm 1910
General Williamson's Diary C Fox Camden Socy 1912
Glimpses of the Olden Times J Carment 1893
Great Diamonds of the World E W Streeter 1882
History of the Reign of Henry VII F. Bacon 1622
History of England A. F. Pollard 1910
London Rediscoveries W G Bell 1929
London under Elizabeth J. Stow ed 1890
Memorials of Westminster Abbey Dean Stanley 1882
Old & New London Magazines 1874
Penny Magazine 1836
Romance of London Timbs 1865
Romance of Treasure Trove C R Beard 1933
State Papers (Colonial)
The Eighteenth Century A Andrews 1865
The Reign of Elizabeth J.B. Black 1935
The Tower of London, R Davey 1910
The Tower of London Lord R. Sutherland-Gower 1901
The Tower of London from Within Sir G. Younghusband 1918
Tower Bills & Records
Tyburn Gallows London County Council 1909
Tyburn Tree A. Marks 1910
Without My Wig Sir T A Jones 1939

We have endeavoured to trace the owners of all copyright material but in certain cases it has proved impossible to do so, and in the event of this book reaching them, we should be glad if they would let us know of any omissions so that we may make proper acknowledgement in future editions.

INDEX

GHOSTS OF THE TOWER OF LONDON
G. ABBOTT

The Tower of London's most horrific tragedies are well known; the gruesome deaths of the two boy princes in the Bloody Tower, the executions of Anne Boleyn, Katherine Howard and Lady Jane Grey, the Jesuit priests and heretics who suffered the agonies of the rack and thumbscrew. Is it any wonder then, that there are frequent reports of blood-curdling screams and moans, of unexplained footsteps and ghostly headless figures? Here, recorded for the first time, is an account for all to read – but preferably not at night – when you only 'think' you're alone!

GREAT ESCAPES FROM THE TOWER OF LONDON
G. ABBOTT

Locked up in the royal prison behind forty foot high walls and the deep encircling moat, guarded by yeoman warders – how could anyone possibly escape? Thousands made no attempt but resigned themselves to their dreaded fate. A few, however, with almost unbelievable ingenuity, succeeded, and their exploits are recounted here by one who, while living in the Tower, had the unique opportunity to research their bids for freedom and to marvel at their achievements.

THE TOWER OF LONDON AS IT WAS
G. ABBOTT

Selected from the author's extensive collection of Victorian and Edwardian postcards of the Tower of London (now in the Guildhall Library, London) these pictures recall days long since gone, before air raids damaged its ancient buildings, before the world's tourists surged in their millions through its archways. Portrayed therein are hansom cabs and top hats, parasols and bustles, with paddle steamers on the Thames, water in the Tower's moat and lions in its Zoo.

BEEFEATERS OF THE TOWER OF LONDON
G. ABBOTT

The yeoman warders, the 'Beefeaters', have been part of the Tower of London for over 900 years and this book tells their complete story; their origins and history, traditions and way of life, weapons and ceremonies, both past and present. Here too are other anecdotes, little known facts and secrets of the ancient fortress; racks and ravens, floods and air raids, murder holes and dungeons; in fact everything you ever wanted to know about the Tower but feared the Axe too much to find out!